"There truly is a CLEANSE for any issue, including anxiety, self-doubt, and trauma healing, no matter what the root cause! I especially love that these techniques are holistic, incorporating mind, body, and soul. This is a book you can refer to and benefit from for the rest of your life."

—Katie Beecher, MS, LPC, Medical Intuitive,
and author of *Heal from Within: A Guidebook to Intuitive Wellness*

"This book will make you want to rise up, stand up, and start believing in yourself and each other. It is a reset for the soul."

—Andrea Owen, author of *Make Some Noise:
Speak Your Mind and Own Your Strength*

"*Emotional Detox Now* from Sherianna Boyle is a book for our times. So many are waking up and realizing that talking about emotional pain often isn't enough to actually change it. With our current climate of constant uncertainty and perpetual change, stress levels are at an all-time high, with disastrous consequences. It is imperative to be able to actually clear emotional stress and energy on a regular basis to have us feeling our best selves. Enter Sherianna's CLEANSE method for hearing, processing, and getting real relief from emotional baggage, presented here in a way that is easy to understand and implement right away! This method is sure to become an essential tool in your toolbox for health and well-being. I'm thrilled this material is being made widely available for practical emotional healing for all."

—Kris Ferraro, healer, coach, and Amazon bestselling
author of *Energy Healing* and *Manifesting*

Emotional Detox Now

Emotional Detox Now

135 SELF-GUIDED PRACTICES TO RENEW YOUR MIND, HEART & SPIRIT

Sherianna Boyle, MED, CAGS

ST. MARTIN'S
ESSENTIALS
NEW YORK

First published in the United States by St. Martin's Essentials, an imprint of St. Martin's Publishing Group

www.stmartins.com

Design by Jonathan Bennett

The Library of Congress Cataloging-in-Publication data is available upon request

ISBN 978-1-250-81741-9 (paper-over-board)
ISBN 978-1-250-80130-2 (ebook)

Our books may be purchased in bulk for promotional, educational, or business use. Please contact your local bookseller or the Macmillan Corporate and Premium Sales Department at 1-800-221-7945, extension 5442, or by email at MacmillanSpecialMarkets@macmillan.com.

First Edition: 2022

10 9 8 7 6 5 4 3 2 1

This book is dedicated to you
and your beautiful emotions.

Your emotions matter, processing them matters even more.

Contents

Part I: Self & Everyday Life

Part III: Family & Home Life

Part IV: Work & Community

Part V: Health & Well-being

VI: Crisis & Tragedy

Author's Note

Dear Reader,

Joy, anger, sadness, fear, love, disliking, and liking . . .
Until now you may have learned about emotions from
their labels, expressing them through physical and spoken
language. I assure you they are much more than that. Your
emotions, when processed, are a form of consciousness,
a vibrational recording if you will, of not only who you
are and the experiences you have had, but who you are
capable of becoming. When emotions are allowed to exist
and are not suppressed or redirected, they tell a story—
sometimes of trauma and pain but also of reconciliation,
healing, love, strength, victory, hope, and more. By
moving through the process in this book you will take
back your right to be the creator of your story.

Welcome to the CLEANSE life!

With love,
Sherianna

All healing happens in the now.

Introduction: All About Emotional Detoxes

I t's been so crazy around here we forgot to order the pizza, so Sheri, if you don't mind, we'd like you to shorten your talk so we can feed everyone first."

"No problem," I said even though I wasn't sure I meant it.

It was early evening and I was at a community school event hosting a workshop on ways to manage stress. Now, with only fifty minutes on the clock and a group of attendees eagerly awaiting my insights, I cut to the chase. "Okay, everyone, we can talk about what is stressing you out and identify all the challenges. I can even give you some quick relief tips and explain the theory behind them. Or we can use this time to CLEANSE. It is up to you—what do you think?"

Nobody in the room had read any of my books and not one of the participants had a clue what I was talking about, but they all chose to CLEANSE.

And we did.

Thirty minutes later, I received so many wonderful comments: *I haven't been this relaxed in a long time . . . When I walked in I had so much on my mind and now I feel like I can handle things . . . I feel a new emotional connection to my wife . . . I came here to learn tips to help my daughter with anxiety and now I realize cleansing was exactly what I needed . . .*

We had a little time left, so I inquired if anyone still wanted to discuss their problems or what was stressing them out. Nobody took me up on it. Instead they asked to continue to acknowledge and sit with the peacefulness that now dwelled within them.

Afterward, I was asked the same question many, many times: How do I CLEANSE on my own? That's when I decided to write this book.

What Do I Mean by CLEANSE?

A CLEANSE is an Emotional Detox, a seven-step practice I created using the acronym C-L-E-A-N-S-E. It stands for:

1. Clear reactivity and neural pathways as you redirect energy by connecting to your body and toning your vagus nerve.

2. Look inward to develop self-awareness and witness your emotions. "I feel . . ."

3. Emit, digest, and physically release emotional energy by engaging with the present by humming.

4. Activate joy (which goes deeper than happiness) via visualization. See it!

5. Nourish, cultivate, and respond with new skills. Embody and experience activated joy.

6. Surrender and let healing flow. "I allow . . ."

7. Ease and trust as you show up for love and life, affirming "I am . . ."

2

Just like a physical detox (think: juice fast or cutting out caffeine and carbs) might alleviate toxicity in your organs, physiological imbalance, or inflammation, an Emotional Detox does the same for your mind. If this seems strange, I totally get it. Most of us are accustomed to thinking of a detox as a method to rinse away the chemicals and impurities we may have absorbed, swallowed, or inhaled. An Emotional Detox is similar, but instead of removing those toxins, you release toxic reactions that prevent you from fully processing your emotions. You won't be purging your emotions per se, but rather the toxic ways you have learned to suppress and repress them. This is because your reactions are preventing emotions from doing what they evolved to do: help you heal, learn, connect to your joyful best self, and grow!

I created the CLEANSE method® of processing, digesting, and releasing negative emotions when I was going through a tough time in my family life. It worked so well for me that I began to share how I CLEANSE with other people through my books and workshops, on podcasts, and in private practice, and it caught on! Cleansing is based on my belief that all emotions are good as long as we process them. In other words, when you CLEANSE, you won't be getting rid of your emotions, you won't be told to "let go," but instead you will learn to see how you react.

Remember, it is our reactions, not the emotions themselves, that lead to tension, conflict, worry, anxiety, and pain. So many of our reactions are rooted in the past—conscious and unconscious memories of emotions that were never fully processed. Before you start sorting through your memories wondering which emotion belongs to which event, know that your reactive patterns aren't just about what may or may not have happened to you, but what you were exposed to, witnessed, or felt. In other words, as emotional beings, we do not just experience our own feelings—we have the capacity to sense unprocessed emotions in others as well. I'm talking about things like anger, anxiety, or fear. The tension you feel around a certain person could be a stuck emotion you need to process or something arising in them. Labeling and blaming doesn't get you anywhere, but cleansing does.

3

Without it, emotions—like a physical illness or even an unhealthy diet—can leave you sluggish, fatigued, drained, unmotivated, and overextended.

I know this from firsthand experience. I'm the kind of person who wakes up in the morning with a chattering, hyperactive monkey mind. My thoughts come so quickly I'm not sure what to focus on first. Sometimes I'm exhausted before I've even gotten out of bed. So rather than check emails, reach for my calendar, or scroll through my social media, I always start my day with a CLEANSE. The moment I begin the first step—Clear—I redirect myself to my body. The thoughts keep rolling, but instead of following their narratives I move to step two— "Having these thoughts first thing in the morning makes me feel . . ." I breath deliberately, inhaling and exhaling through my nose. Once I move through all seven steps, the chatter ceases or at least grows quieter, allowing me to focus (without much effort) on one task at a time. What I have learned through years of this practice is many of my unprocessed emotions show up first thing in the morning, ready to be cleared for the day. To keep it accessible, I included a sample of this morning CLEANSE, at the end under "Bonus."

Once you try CLEANSE for yourself you will realize it works. You will see everything in a new light because as you move through and beyond clearing congested, stagnant energy caused by suppression of emotions you will open doors to a new way of having relationships and experiences. You will also see that even if the situation I describe does not apply to you in the moment, you may be drawn to it because at one point in your life or in your genetic line it applied to someone or something. In other words, let go of trying to match yourself with each CLEANSE and just allow yourself to go through the motions. Trust, as you CLEANSE, you will stop judging what is happening to you or blaming yourself and the people around you for your "bad" feelings. Instead, you will embrace every moment as an opportunity to develop skills, wisdom, and insight while gaining clarity, peace, and higher knowing. Right now . . .

To make this as simple and as easy as possible, and so you will really CLEANSE and not just think about doing it, I've written this book in an accessible and prescriptive way. If you want to learn more about the science and psychology of the CLEANSE method you can find tons of information in my other books (especially *Emotional Detox*) and on my website, but this book is a tool you can use when you are confronted with a specific problem and need a CLEANSE to work through it, often right away! In other words, clear reactivity now and analyze it later with clarity and grounding. Some of you may also want to work your way through this book one CLEANSE at a time and take a proactive approach to your personal development. Pick the way that is best for you using the 135 CLEANSEs here, which I have grouped into six categories:

1. Self & Everyday Life

2. Love & Relationships

3. Family & Home Life

4. Work & Community

5. Health & Well-being

6. Crisis & Tragedy

I recognized there is a vast difference between the power of the emotions that surface when dealing with something like the behavior of an annoying coworker and those that overwhelm us when we are blindsided by grief, but those little reactions add up and develop into big ones over time. It might not seem as important to process the emotions around our everyday experiences, but truly it is. If you CLEANSE the smaller stuff as it comes up you will be more resilient and better able to handle the big stuff when it arises.

Each CLEANSE presents the process in manageable pieces, using situations and examples most of us can relate to that are designed to reveal unprocessed, stuck, or even festering emotions. The Emotional Detox mindset is the foundation for this practice and the CLEANSE steps are the tools. Remember: Emotions do not disempower you; ignoring them, stuffing them down, or holding them back does. Think of emotions as the symptoms and the CLEANSE as the medicine.

Cleansing 101

STEP ONE: CLEAR REACTIVITY

When we Clear, we open the pathway for emotions to flow. This launches the detox by letting your body know you are choosing to feel and heal both physically and emotionally. The purpose of step one is to eliminate as much embodied and deep-rooted emotional reactivity as possible so that you can access the actual emotions. Emotional reactivity can be most recognized by the fight, fright, fix, or freeze response. It is the feeling inside your body that makes you want to do, change, or escape from something. Emotional reactivity often manifests from unresolved emotions and misunderstandings from childhood. In other words, as a child you might have felt like you did something wrong and dealt with the feeling by becoming defensive (fight), staying away from the person who was upset (fright), trying to make the situation better (fix), or disassociate from the moment (freeze) as a way to control the fear and pain.

Think of Clear like updating your computer software so that all your internal programs reflect the beliefs, thoughts, feelings you are looking to create today, ones such as happiness, love, compassion, healing, and more. I find this step to be both loving and reassuring. You are letting your nervous system know you are choosing to process (rather than revisit an old experience of) a feeling. Without this step, you could stir up old memories. Reliving the triggering ones may cause you to resort to deep-seated and unsuccessful ways of avoiding or wrestling with old emotions, or worse, you might retraumatize yourself. Step one tells your body, "I hear you . . . I validate you . . . I reassure you my intention is to process (rather than repeat) what is causing discomfort or pain."

The technique I find best for accessing and eliminating reactivity involves the vagus nerve. It is the longest nerve of the human body's automatic nervous system, beginning at the brain stem, branching through the heart, lungs, abdomen, and ending at the colon—all places where unprocessed emotions are stored and can manifest as physical conditions. You've likely felt this when your heart raced in fear; you were so upset you could not catch your breath; or an upsetting experience made you nauseous or affected your digestion. As you will see in the CLEANSEs, I recommend different techniques for different issues.

You can begin to access and tone your vagus nerve by:

1. Pressing acupressure points

2. Stretching

3. Breath work

4. Mudras

PRESSING ACUPRESSURE POINTS

Think of these points as your reset buttons—not stopping or canceling emotions but redirecting them.

- Take the two peace-sign fingers of your dominant hand and press about an inch above your navel. Shift the pressure slightly to the right and then slightly to the left. These are your three acupressure points.

- Then, using two fingers of your nondominant hand, touch the lowest point of the crown of your head while pressing the center, right, and, left points near your navel with the dominant hand.

- Move the fingers of your nondominant hand to the middle of the crown as you continue to press the points on your abdomen.

- Move your nondominant hand upward and closer to your forehead while continuing to press the points near your navel.

As you will see, this is not the only way to tone your vagus nerve—many CLEANSEs give you alternative options—but it is the easiest and most accessible one. When I tone my vagus nerve in the morning I tend to do the three presses along with a neck stretch. I practice the other variations you will see in this book at other times during the day. Remember: The point is to have options when it comes to step one.

STRETCHING

Stretching your neck and spine stimulates the vagus nerve.

- I recommend standing or even sitting tall, with your feet hip-width apart.

- Tilt your right ear toward your right shoulder, which will naturally unclench your jaw.

- Repeat on the left side and as you do remember to breathe fully—inhale and exhale.

BREATH WORK

The average person takes between ten and twenty breaths per minute. Toning the vagus nerve will slow down your breathing, but most of us need to learn how to do this. If you have a mind-body practice you like such as yoga, tai chi, or breath-focused meditation you can use that to reset your vagus nerve. Otherwise, try this simple method called ratio breathing:

- Inhale for two counts . . . *one, two* . . . as you soften and inflate your belly (not your chest).

- Exhale . . . *one, two* . . . and sense how your navel moves toward your spine.

- Repeat!

- As you grow comfortable with the practice add to the count . . . four breaths, maybe six.

MUDRAS

Mudras are ancient hand positions, which when held and paired with your breath assist the movement of energy throughout your entire

8

body. You might be familiar with images of yogis holding up both hands, forefingers touching thumbs, in an "okay" sign—that's a mudra. So is putting your hands together in prayer position. Mudras are simple and easy to use. A few of them show up in the CLEANSEs that follow.

STEP TWO: LOOK INWARD

When we look inward, we witness our emotions with an "I feel" statement, which we support with the breath. This loosens the emotions you are storing so they can be more easily cleared in step three. Looking inward begins "How I feel in my body right now is . . ." The goal here is to raise the question and just observe the response versus finishing or answering the statement. Each stem sentence is intended to be stated out loud and then followed by one inhale and one exhale. And then you finish the sentence as you intentionally inhale and exhale, usually through your nose. As will see, each specific CLEANSE recommends different variations of the "I feel" statement.

I encourage you to frame your step-two statements in the present tense, even if the things you are cleansing happened in the past. This is because all healing begins in the now. Do not worry about figuring out how to go about this because, as you will see, I have done the groundwork for you. Your job is simply to be open to the process. You may find it interesting, like I do, how much we have been trained to answer (or think about how we will answer) things verbally by giving feelings a label. Learning how to ask yourself how you feel and replying with your breath instead of definitions or explanations takes feeling to a radical and exciting new level.

This is so important it bears repeating: When it comes to the looking-inward statement, do not answer the question, allow your breath (both the inhale and exhale) to respond. If thoughts arise, that's fine, know they are coming up because emotions are being processed. Stay with your breath and allow it to tell the story. Soon you may find, like so many of my clients, how much your thoughts about your emotions and the natural tendency to talk about or justify them may be getting in the way of processing them. Unprocessed emotions can

9

lead to inner turmoil, angst, distractibility, and forgetfulness, while processed emotions do the opposite, becoming the source for calm, stability, clarity, focus, good judgment, and strength.

STEP THREE: EMIT

Now comes the magic! When we emit, we produce a sound. Many healing and spiritual modalities use this technique—from the yogi's "om" to the psychotherapist's primal scream. I like to work with an exhaled hum. The physical vibration from the hum has an overall cleansing and soothing effect, teaching our body how to regulate emotions and transform them.

Some tips for accessing the power of your hum:

- Sit or stand up tall with your feet hip-width apart. If you are hunched over, lopsided, or tilted, your diaphragm might be compressed, impacting the quality of your hum.

- Do not cross your legs or arms. This helps provide grounding for your body and allows energy to flow.

- Try your best to extend your hum for as long as you can. To do this, you will want to inhale through your nose first and then on exhale produce a nice long hum (three to five counts) navel pressing toward your spine.

- It is best to hum aloud. You do not have to belt it out, but your hum should be audible (at least to you). In fact, sometimes louder humming can be less effective. You want your hum to run deep into the core of your body, so that you can feel the vibration deep within your inner organs. Allowing your hum to be long and drawn out will support the process. Exhale fully.

- Between hums, take a deep breath to inflate your lungs, making sure to inhale naturally, not forcing it. Forced inhales can sometimes make you dizzy, so if this occurs you might want to slow down a bit.

- In almost every CLEANSE, you will do three hums. There are a few occasions when I will suggest more, so be sure to read each step thoroughly to get the most out of your CLEANSE.

STEP FOUR: ACTIVATE JOY

To activate joy (which I define as a state of expansiveness) you visualize an image of the qualities you wish to cultivate—usually the opposite of the feeling that led you to the CLEANSE in the first place. If you are irritable you would visualize patience; if you are feeling undeserving you would visualize receiving appreciation—whatever it is you wish to increase or cultivate in your life. If you are having a day where you cannot seem to visualize, no worries, I have offered lots of suggestions in each CLEANSE so that you can continue to move through and not get stuck. Know it is okay to not always feel connected to your CLEANSE—it is the intention that counts. Think of my guidance as the two of us doing the practice together as I coach you and suggest images. Trust the process and see it!

To activate joy:

1. Redirect your attention from the vibration of your hum to the feeling you want to instill within yourself. Do this by visualizing it in your mind's eye—imagine what the feeling would look and be like. For example, what would calm look like? Where would you be? What would you see? Smell? Hear?

2. In some spiritual practices, the mind's eye is called the third eye—said to be located in the space between your eyebrows. It is believed to connect to and affect your pineal gland, which is located deep within the center of the brain. The pineal gland influences hormonal function, especially the production of melatonin, which modulates sleep, and along with your hypothalamus, helps regulate emotions.

11

3. As we visualize, we begin to open our heart center in the middle of the chest (where the heart chakra is in yoga). This cleanses the atmosphere both within and outside of us, allowing joy to pervade and prevail.

When it comes to activating joy there are no fixed rules. I provide you with guidance in each CLEANSE, but if another visualization arises, let that happen. You're receiving valuable insight, so go with what feels right for you. I will support you along the way. Whatever image shows up is exactly what you need, no matter how silly or arbitrary it may seem. It is important to not judge but, rather, to experience.

STEP FIVE: NOURISH

When we nourish, cultivate, and respond we feel what we see. This can be through our sense of smell (the salt air at the beach), hearing (birds chirping), or sensation (a light breeze on your face). Think of steps four and five as a pair. In step four, you visualize what you are creating, and then in step five, you allow yourself to experience it in your body as if it were happening. The amazing thing is, when you do this, your body responds as if it really were!

When you nourish, you further detox emotions by assimilating the joy we activated (via your visualization) into your physical, emotional, and even spiritual bodies. It is a way of refilling a depleted energy bank. As you do, you become more relaxed, centered, and equanimous. You embody what you've visualized.

To nourish:

1. Allow yourself to experience your visualizations through feeling.

2. Observe, appreciate, and permit inner movement to take place in your body.

3. Notice how your breathing elongates or deepens with the

process and how relaxation increases. This is a state from which you will learn how to communicate and connect.

4. Pause for a moment and observe your body. Notice your inhale and exhale. Notice your sense of connection to others and the world around you.

STEP SIX: SURRENDER

Surrendering not only frees us from the need to control our emotions, it is an affirmation that we are choosing to allow these visualizations and feelings (sensations) to become part of our experience as physical beings. It is no different from saying, "I allow myself to have more of this." Your choice is an act of free will coming from a state of processing your emotions, and this is what makes the Surrender step so powerful. Allowing something from a low vibration (like fear or anger) is one thing, however; allowing it from a higher vibration (like love or joy) is a whole different level of experience. The first five steps got you here and your vibrations (sensations) are much higher than before you began your CLEANSE.

When we surrender we make an "allow" statement. This can be done in one of two ways:

1. State the feeling or state of being you desire. Words like "freedom," "love," "peace," and "strength" are often used in allow statements.

2. State the opposite of how you have been reacting or coping. For example, if you are tired of having to defend yourself to others, your allow statement might be: "I allow self-acceptance. I allow agreement. I allow connection."

Whichever kind of allow statement you utilize, remember to always:

• **Breathe between each allow statement.**

• **Speak from your gut or core.**

- **Present it as a statement, not a question.**

- **Steady your gaze as you embody direction, not haziness.**

In the last step we make an "I am" statement that completes the CLEANSE as we become present in mind, body, and spirit—this is ease and trust. You've prepped your body with step one, acknowledged your emotions (without rehashing them) in step two, supplied yourself with energy by humming in step three, and channeled this energy toward what you choose to create (see, feel, and allow) in steps four, five, and six. Now you are ready to integrate these processes from something you do or see outside of yourself (perhaps the image of a beautiful waterfall or a street with only green traffic lights) to the understanding that what you see is you—the flow and power of a waterfall, the moving easily through a run of green lights. In other words, we are not separate from ease, we are ease. Ease lives inside of you, not outside of you. The seventh step provides an opportunity to strengthen your connection to who you are, and as you do that you begin to see you are far more capable than you may have imagined before you began the CLEANSE.

Think of the Ease step as merging your "I am" with the joy frequency:

I am (state of processing your emotions) + joy (state of expansion) = oneness

Being in a state of oneness builds a foundation of confidence, faith, and trust—not just trust in others, but also in yourself. Living a life with ease means you are aware of your choices and you are on the path of least resistance. Living in the "I am" means you are choosing to love unconditionally. When you choose to feel rather than react, you are deciding to love. It is that simple. Ease is knowing you can convert the frequency of any emotion—anger, sadness, frustration, confusion, or anxiety—into something new: forgiveness. You no longer need to merely cope, and that is freeing.

Some Tips for Moving Through the CLEANSE Process

- Always read the introduction to the CLEANSE first, even if you do not think it applies to you. The stories I share are intentional, and I'm hoping they will loosen or elicit buried emotions.

- Begin with the first step and follow each in the exact sequence. Each CLEANSE takes between five and fifteen minutes. If you get distracted—let's say the phone rings or the dog needs to go out— take care of what you need to do and return to where you left off.

- Although each CLEANSE is designed to go in order from step one (each step builds upon the one before), they are flexible. So if you need to, you can linger on one step, or pause, break away, and return to the process.

- If you are having difficulty working through a CLEANSE, try slowing down and spending time with step one (Clear) as you may be rushing to the other steps.

- Give yourself permission to take your time; this is not a race. One way to know if you are ready for step two is when your breathing feels natural—an inhale flowing into an exhale, not one and then the other.

- Keep this book handy (maybe in your car or on your bedside table) to build your practice and so you have a tool to use whenever tough emotional situations come up or persistent ones overwhelm you.

- You may choose to work with this book day by day, page by page, one CLEANSE at a time, until you get through all 135 practices—like a thorough emotional scrub down and purification. You might turn to a section that applies to what is showing up in your life right this minute—something you need to process immediately like disappointment, anger, or grief— and select that specific CLEANSE. No matter what you choose,

15

the most important thing is to keep at it. Everybody needs to CLEANSE something!

- Make cleansing a ritual. Even if there is no particular issue, consider sitting in a special chair, lighting a candle, or going through the steps at approximately the same time of day as you work through the book. You never know what might arise or get digested!

About Emotions

It is possible you may not yet be sure what it is like to truly feel an emotion. You're not the only one! I have taught the CLEANSE method to lots of people who have been trained since childhood to keep emotions in check or to view them as signs that something about themselves has to be fixed or managed rather than felt. Sometimes not feeling your feelings looks like stoicism, not wanting to be a vulnerable, or a deep-seated sense of unworthiness. You may inwardly believe revealing or even discussing what you feel will make you a burden or appear weak or insecure, so why bother?

I totally get it, I was there too, and now I refer to that time as my pre-CLEANSE life. You will know you're feeling an emotion and not squelching or labeling it when you can have a thought (even a negative one) and not be triggered by it. Instead you will be able to witness your thoughts and experiences without attaching to them. Should you veer from the path of feeling your emotions (as we all do from time to time), these three points will guide you back:

1. Processing your emotions won't hurt you, but resisting them will!

2. Feel first, then if necessary, communicate the way you feel.

3. Always CLEANSE before any major decisions or actions—like ending a relationship.

4. Take your time with the CLEANSE and remember, your emotions matter and processing them matters most.

16

What you will experience as you move through a CLEANSE is how thinking and talking are different from feeling. Feeling gives you energy while thinking and talking (without awareness) tend to sap your energy or give you a temporary boost that does not last. This is when a CLEANSE can come in handy. The CLEANSE method has taught me so many things and has truly made a difference in my life and the lives of my friends and clients. I'm thrilled to be able to share it with you, so welcome to the CLEANSE journey!

What you resist constricts.

Part I

The way I see it, is there are two versions of you—before and after a CLEANSE. The first is in a state of reactivity and the other is calm, resilient, and expansive.

Here is what the CLEANSE has taught me: judgment is the root of all obstacles. You see, when you tell me you have lost your voice or you feel powerless, I know there is a part of you that is judging yourself. If you feel like others do not respect you, there is a part of you that does not fully respect yourself. If you are surrounded by people who treat you unfairly, there is an aspect of you that does not value yourself. This is because we are all connected—sometimes on a conscious level, but often on a subconscious one—and the sooner we realize that, the closer we will be to understanding what it looks and feels like to experience peace and ease in our lives. This well-being begins with the self and radiates outward to our families, communities, and ultimately the world.

These CLEANSEs for self and everyday life address the various ways you may be reacting to what is showing up both inside and outside of you. Your external self might be interpreted as your identity—how you believe the world sees and labels you. Your inner self includes the ways you respond to those perceptions, your reactions to your thoughts, as well as the ways you manage stress, deal with your emotions, and cope with your unconscious and conscious memories.

I once asked a young client of mine what it felt like to live with labels of obsessive-compulsive disorder, anxiety, and attention deficit hyperactivity disorder. Her response was, "I feel validated, yet the same." In other words, the labels helped her communicate to others what she was feeling and going through, but it would not be until she started her CLEANSE journey that she was able to begin to fully understand herself. While it might seem like society has told you that you are not good enough, your feelings are wrong or problematic, or you have to achieve more, a CLEANSE challenges you to tune inward and discover who you truly are and what you are capable of beyond the reactivity, descriptions, and expectations.

Cleansing Self-Sabotage

*Y*ou lost the weight you wanted to shed only to let unhealthy foods creep back into your diet. You have every intention of quitting smoking but still sneak "just one" cigarette when nobody is around and can't quite kick the habit. You know you should extricate yourself from that destructive relationship, but you reply to texts you should probably ignore.

These are examples of self-sabotage. Think of it as a behavior that interferes with your long-term goals. It is not as if you wake up in the morning and announce, "I am going to sabotage myself today by calling my ex so they can make me feel bad about myself" or "I am going to eat that pint of ice cream even though I know I'll feel awful." Self-sabotage usually happens unconsciously, right? This is because habits (both good and bad) get established in our brains.

The good news is, thanks to neuroplasticity—the brain's ability to form and reorganize synaptic connections—you can rewire and change your brain and therefore break and redirect a bad habit. The bottom line is bad habits are patterns of reactivity. They are ways you have learned to suppress your emotional energy. In fact, I am going to go out on a limb and say self-sabotage is a sign you have mastered and established a habit so well that your body actually prefers it. Sometimes we mistake habits for our external identity: *I'm a person who can't stop eating sweets. I'm someone who always chooses relationships with people who demean me.* To CLEANSE your attachments to old ways of reacting, so you won't binge-eat when you are worried or text your ex even though you know it will make you feel awful, I suggest you practice this CLEANSE whenever self-destructive urges occur.

Clear Reactivity Begin by balling your fists really hard, scrunching your shoulders up toward your ears, and squeezing the muscles of your face. Hold this posture for the count of one . . . two . . . three . . . and release. Allow the blood to flow through the rest of your body, breathe, and move to step two.

Look Inward How I feel in my body right now is . . . inhale through your nose . . . exhale through your nose.

Having these urges makes me feel . . . inhale . . . exhale . . .

Observing these urges in this way now makes me feel . . . inhale . . . exhale . . .

Emit Hum three times.

Activate See it! Visualize an image of releasing, relinquishing, or neutralizing. Perhaps a cup of watered-down coffee; the taste was so bland you no longer wanted another sip.

Nourish Feel it! Imagine placing the coffee down, brushing your teeth so you now have a nice minty taste in your mouth, and going outside into the fresh air.

Surrender Say: "I allow fresh. I allow renewal. I allow release. I allow freedom."

Ease Say: "I am pure. I am refreshed. I am renewed. I am love. I am whole. I am free."

Cleansing
Avoidance

Have you ever dragged your feet? Maybe you delayed showing up to a social gathering, kept rescheduling a dental appointment, or always found a reason to skip your workout. You know it is important to connect with friends and family, take care of those molars, or move your body, yet you manage to postpone or ignore these activities.

Maybe you keep putting off a conversation with your partner or friend that really needs to happen? You realize it is time to tell someone how you feel or how they hurt you, yet each time the slightest opportunity arises to communicate you lose the courage to speak up. Buried feelings can gnaw at you, leaving you emotionally depleted. Avoidance is a reaction, just like not choosing is a choice, but fortunately it can be cleansed.

Clear Reactivity Holding your peace-sign fingers about an inch apart, press your fingertips directly above your navel. Be sure to sit up tall. Tilt your head side to side, your right ear toward your right shoulder, your left ear toward your left shoulder. Breathe.

Look Inward How I feel in my body right now is . . . inhale through your nose . . . exhale through your nose.

Resisting makes me feel . . . inhale . . . exhale . . .

When my nerves or self-doubt get in the way, it makes me feel . . . inhale . . . exhale . . .

Acknowledging and sharing my thoughts and feelings now makes me . . . inhale . . . exhale . . .

Emit Hum three times.

Activate See it! Visualize a scene that evokes joy, acceptance, applause, delight, and enthusiasm. See and hear people cheering and celebrating you.

Nourish Feel it! Imagine the vibration of the applause, how your body begins to move upright with the encouragement.

Surrender Say: "I allow courage. I allow joy. I allow acceptance. I allow presence. I allow delight. I allow freedom."

Ease Say: "I am delight. I am courage. I am present. I am joy. I am free."

Cleansing Excuses

Have you ever apologized for somebody else's actions? Maybe you tolerated a slight or insult that was inappropriate or unacceptable? When we excuse others from taking responsibility for their own behaviors we rob them of the opportunity to discover their capabilities and be their best selves.

On the other hand, if you are the one making excuses—meaning you are quick to apologize, you explain away your feelings, or you tell yourself you are not capable of something—this is your chance to acknowledge and CLEANSE these behaviors.

Without a CLEANSE, excuses may redirect or obscure emotions. While that might feel good in the short term, without the awareness you receive from processing emotions fully you never get the chance to complete and move beyond old ways of thinking and reacting and grow.

Clear Reactivity Straighten your arms out in front of you, turn the backs of your hands toward each other. After holding that position, move your arms apart and sweep them to the back of your body. Interlace your fingers as best you can as you open and extend your chest. Hold that stretch for a count of one . . . two . . . three . . . and release.

Look Inward How I feel in my body right now is . . . inhale through your nose . . . exhale through your nose.

When I make excuses I feel . . . inhale . . . exhale . . .

When I catch myself defending inappropriate behavior, it makes me feel . . . inhale . . . exhale . . .

Seeing accountability and managing my emotions in this way makes me feel . . . inhale . . . exhale . . .

Emit Hum three times.

Activate See it! Visualize the act of curiosity—perhaps traveling to a place you have always wanted to visit. Imagine what it would look like and what questions you would ask the locals about where to eat, what to do, and which sights to see.

Nourish Feel it! Experience in your body what it is like to ask for and want to know more. You might sense a slight flutter like a butterfly in your chest.

Surrender Say: "I allow questions. I allow energy. I allow curiosity. I allow movement. I allow strength."

Ease Say: "I am strong. I am questioning. I am curious. I am wonder. I am energy. I am clarity. I am support. I am free."

Cleansing Self-Inflicted Pressure

Do you put a lot of pressure on yourself? No matter how hard you work or what you accomplish, does it seem like you could always do better? Or maybe you feel overwhelmed and exhausted by all your worrisome thoughts. Perhaps you are obsessing about the future and forgetting the value of being in the now. If so, you may want to ask yourself if you are comparing yourself to someone or something? For example, if your neighbor paints their house, does that put pressure on you to paint yours? Do you feel your boss won't appreciate you if you do not work past the point of exhaustion? Maybe you have filled your time with so many tasks and responsibilities that you have little or no time to relax or have fun. Or maybe you have allowed others' expectations of you to obscure what you are realistically able to do or actually want to do. If so, it is time to CLEANSE.

Clear Reactivity Take your hands and press all your fingers together in prayer position keeping the palms apart. Close your eyes and breathe softly through your nose . . . inhaling . . . exhaling.

Look Inward How I feel in my body right now is . . . inhale through your nose . . . exhale through your nose.

When the energy gets tight in my body, it makes me feel . . . inhale . . . exhale . . .

Having all this pressing on my mind now makes me feel . . . inhale . . . exhale . . .

Emit Hum three times.

Activate See it! Visualize a scene that evokes lightness, loosening, calm, relief, and freedom.

Nourish Feel it! Imagine loosening a tight lid on a bottle. Perhaps it is a refreshing bottle of cool water. Remove the cap and imagine what it would be like to drink it now.

Surrender Say: "I allow relief. I allow loosening. I allow freedom. I allow calm."

Ease Say: "I am love. I am joy. I am calm. I am safe. I am free."

Cleansing Inadequacy

Sometimes we put too much pressure on ourselves because we are feeling inadequate. It might happen when you join a singing group and find out your voice is not as trained as the rest of the ensemble. Maybe you weren't chosen for a team or you were dating someone who broke up with you to date someone else. Maybe you are a parent and it seems like everyone else is doing a better job with their kids. Things like this bring up feelings of not being good enough. Face it, everybody gets down in the dumps sometimes! Without a regular CLEANSE, life can begin to feel like a battle or a competition you can't win.

Before you give up or tell yourself it is hopeless, recognize you have emotions that need to be processed. Underneath the story of not being good enough may be unresolved reactions of rejection, disappointment, and sadness. We have all encountered these feelings at some point in our lives. The question is, have you really allowed yourself to process them? If you find yourself in situations where you feel weak, less-than, small, or limited, then it is likely this CLEANSE is for you.

Clear Reactivity Laugh a big belly laugh. Yes, you read that correctly: laugh. Go ahead and lift the corners of your mouth, smile wide, and soon you will find that your entire body wants to join in. That wasn't so bad, was it?

Look Inward How I feel in my body right now is . . . inhale through your nose . . . exhale through your nose.

When I tell myself it is my fault or I am not good enough, it makes me feel . . . inhale . . . exhale.

Carrying this heaviness inside me now makes me feel . . . inhale . . . exhale.

Emit Hum three times.

Activate See it! Visualize something wholesome, pure, sincere, and honest. Perhaps a white dove or a cooing baby.

Nourish Feel it! Imagine that wholesome experience, what it is like to be in the presence of an authentic, nonjudgmental, loving energy.

Surrender Say: "I allow energy. I allow pure. I allow love. I allow wholesome. I allow worthy."

Ease Say: "I am worthy. I am energy. I am love. I am forgiving. I am enough. I am free."

Cleansing Making Mistakes

There has never been anyone who has not made a mistake. Ever. I know I have. Perhaps you misjudged or misread someone else's behavior? Maybe you forgot to give someone the credit they deserved? Maybe you sent that angry email too soon or were impatient with your child or insensitive to your partner? These things can cause a lot of unresolved guilt and frustration and a relentless litany of "I should have . . ." or "I wish I had . . ." in your mind.

This is important: Before beginning this CLEANSE do not focus on cleansing the mistake—you can't undo what has been done—but instead you will focus on cleansing *your reaction* to that mistake. As strange as this may sound, the way I look at it is the mistake gave you an opportunity to process some emotions that might not have been revealed otherwise. You see, mistakes tend to bring up some of those intense emotional memories we may have buried—perhaps a time when you felt a powerful sense of failure or disappointment. In this CLEANSE be sure to give some extra attention to your hum. I will guide you to go a little deeper when we get there.

Clear Reactivity Tone your vagus nerve by tilting your right ear toward your right shoulder as you gently press your tongue on the roof of your mouth and exhale through your nose . . . one . . . two . . . three. Bring your head back to center. Now, tilt your left ear toward your left shoulder and again gently press your tongue on the roof of your mouth and exhale through your nose . . . one . . . two . . . three.

Look Inward How I feel in my body right now is . . . inhale through your nose . . . exhale through your nose.

When I realized what I did was wrong, it made me feel . . . inhale . . . exhale . . .

When I realized it was too late, it made me feel . . . inhale . . . exhale . . .

The thought of screwing up makes me feel . . . inhale . . . exhale . . .

Emit Hum three times. As you do, concentrate on clearing reactions such as over-apologizing, denial, or blame. Imagine rubbing them away with the vibration of your hum.

Activate See it! Visualize a delightful piece of scenery such as a charming garden, an enchanting forest, or a pleasant sunny day by the ocean.

Nourish Feel it! Imagine your body's sensations on that pleasant day, full of unexpected surprises.

Surrender Say: "I allow delightful. I allow charming. I allow pleasant. I allow contented."

Ease Say: "I am delightful. I am charming. I am pleasant. I am happy. I am free."

Cleansing When You Feel You Don't Fit In

It is normal and natural to want to be accepted by others. It may be a certain group of friends or colleagues or the opportunity to share an activity you enjoy. It might be your own family or someone else's. But what if you don't jive with the people in this group? Sure, you might have a few things in common, however, there may be aspects of the other members you are not crazy about. Or maybe you feel like you're left out of their inside jokes. That sense of not belonging can really gnaw at you. So what do you do? Do you try to fit in and make the best of the situation? Or do you accept that you are different? You won't fully know the answer to these questions until you process the emotions waiting to be digested.

Clear Reactivity Give the back of your head a yummy massage using fingers. Reach under your hairline and knead the bottom ridge where the nape of your neck meets your skull. Do this for at least one minute.

Look Inward How I feel in my body right now is . . . inhale through your nose . . . exhale through your nose.

Trying to fit into this group or situation makes me feel . . . inhale . . . exhale . . .

When my efforts do not pay off, it makes me feel . . . inhale . . . exhale . . .

Letting go of trying to fit in makes me feel . . . inhale . . . exhale . . .

Emit Hum three times.

Activate See it! Visualize a scene that represents promise, joy, calm, authenticity, and love. Perhaps beautiful marine life—colorful fish, coral, and shells under sparkling water.

Nourish Feel it! Imagine the sensation of being around pure, genuine love and joy. You might experience this with a parent, grandparent, a significant adult in your life, or maybe even your dog or cat.

Surrender Say: "I allow transparency. I allow genuineness. I allow approval. I allow joy."

Ease Say: "I am transparent. I am genuine. I am authentic. I am approval. I am acceptance. I am joy."

Cleansing When You Hear Yourself Saying, "Yeah . . . Yeah . . ."

"Yeah" is a casual way of saying yes and if you repeat the word "yeah" several times in a row, it can be similar to nodding your head in numb agreement. If you were to pause and really tune in to what is coming up emotionally you might find a feeling of being rushed, distracted, or maybe trying to do too many things at once. I have uttered my fair share of "yeah" in the past, but these days I am not so quick to overlook them. "Yeah" without awareness can be a way of suppressing anxiety and feelings of being overwhelmed. Repeating the word "yeah" aloud can be a way to buffer and manage your situation, a way to delay taking action. While "yeah" can serve you in the moment and sometimes help you stay on track, I suggest you pay attention to that little word. It may be a sign of impatience, annoyance, denial, or preoccupation that is coming up to be processed.

Clear Reactivity Stand up tall. Place your feet hip-width apart and march in place for about thirty seconds. Go ahead and lift your knees high and swing your arms back and forth as you march. (You can modify this exercise if you need to stay seated.)

Look Inward How I feel in my body right now is . . . inhale through your nose . . . exhale through your nose.

Rushing makes me feel . . . inhale . . . exhale . . .

When I shorten and speed up my words or do not pay full attention to the people around me, it makes me feel . . . inhale . . . exhale . . .

When others interrupt or distract me, it makes me feel . . . inhale . . . exhale . . .

Emit Hum three times. Try your best to extend your humming a bit and make it last a little longer than usual.

Activate See it! Visualize something calm, patient, soft, flexible, and nourishing. Perhaps a silky flower petal.

Nourish Feel it! Imagine touching the flower petal gently with your fingertips. Sense and appreciate the softness.

Surrender Say: "I allow soft. I allow patient. I allow gentle. I allow calm. I allow presence."

Ease Say: "I am calm. I am present. I am focused. I am gentle. I am soft."

Cleansing Insecurity

Have you been comparing, measuring your accomplishments (and maybe even your happiness) against other people's lately? Are you focusing on your perceived flaws? Do you feel like you are hiding, covering yourself up, making yourself small? If so, you have something to CLEANSE. You can recognize insecurity and its parallel low self-esteem by its qualities of inner tension, irritability, dread, and nervousness. Here is the thing: Insecurity when left unrecognized can turn into a coping mechanism. In other words, as long as you feel insecure and you have some way of expressing or showing this to others—such as looking down at the floor, sitting alone, or always letting other people dominate a situation—then you do not have to go through the discomfort of moving through the emotions that are coming to be processed. Strange but true, insecurity can actually be a way of managing your fear of success, judgment, intimacy, failure, and more. So if you want to move through it and activate joy, this CLEANSE is for you!

Clear Reactivity Start by opening up your emotional pathways from the base of your skull to your tailbone by activating your spine. Try a few cat-cow stretches from yoga. You can do this by getting on your hands and knees in a tabletop position. Tilt your head and tailbone up at the same time as you inhale through your nose. On the exhale, tuck your chin and tailbone as you press your navel toward your spine. Then sit up straight and complete the rest of your CLEANSE.

Look Inward How I feel in my body right now is . . . inhale through your nose . . . exhale through your nose or mouth—whatever feels most natural and most calming to you right now. (Try both and see what you think.)

When I compare myself to others, it makes me feel . . . inhale . . . exhale . . .

Noticing my flaws makes me feel . . . inhale . . . exhale . . .

When I think of what I could be capable of, it makes me feel . . . inhale . . . exhale . . .

Emit Hum three times.

Activate See it! Visualize something in nature that represents strength, confidence, possibilities, and reassurance—a mountain or a tall, sturdy oak tree.

Nourish Feel it! Flood your body with the force of this image—its stability and confidence.

Surrender Say: "I allow strength. I allow trust. I allow ease. I allow security. I allow confidence."

Ease Say: "I am strength. I am trusting. I am secure. I am confident. I am capable. I am ease."

Cleansing Feeling Tricked or Misled

I once had a client who was hired for a new job. She was so excited! Or she was until she received her contract from her company and discovered it had a different salary from what she'd been promised. The man who hired her fully acknowledged the discrepancy, and then tried to convince my client how lucky she was to be getting the job at all—even at the lower rate! This is an example of being tricked. She was told one thing, but actions did not reflect it. You might relate to being deceived by someone who cheated romantically, someone who broke a promise, or someone you supported politically who let you and your community down. Maybe you even "got over" it. While these events might seem like old stories or the kinds of situations that happen to everyone, without processing the emotions connected to them we risk repeating patterns and cycles of reactivity. However, that will end when you choose to CLEANSE.

Clear Reactivity Splashing icy water on your face is a great way to tone your vagus nerve. If you do not want to get too wet, use a cold compress. Do this for thirty seconds.

Look Inward How I feel in my body right now is . . . inhale through your nose . . . exhale through your nose.

When I realized I had been lied to or things weren't as they seemed, it made me feel . . . inhale . . . exhale . . .

Repeat: When I realized I was lied to or things were not as they seemed, it made me feel . . . inhale . . . exhale . . .

When I am not honest with myself, I feel . . . inhale . . . exhale . . .

Emit Hum three times.

Activate See it! Visualize something in nature that illustrates relief, support, help, or assistance. It can be as simple as the gift of a gentle breeze on a hot sticky day or sunlight illuminating a path out of the forest.

Nourish Feel it! Imagine experiencing that gentle breeze, how you might close your eyes as the cool, refreshing air blows against your skin.

Surrender Say: "I allow gratitude. I allow aid. I allow relief. I allow support. I allow honesty. I allow love."

Ease Say: "I am assistance. I am love. I am authentic. I am vulnerable. I am honest. I am stable. I am free."

Cleansing for Self-Forgiveness

Maybe you blew up at your partner or child. Maybe you let someone down at work or didn't show up for them when they really needed you. Maybe you unintentionally hurt a friend's feelings. Today is your day to receive the beautiful, liberating energy of forgiveness! Forgiving yourself doesn't happen by force, it happens by feeling. By simply allowing this process to begin in even the tiniest way, you open up the doorway to letting an incredibly powerful healing energy enter. Do not turn back now. Keep going, keep opening, otherwise you run the risk of dishonoring the part of yourself that is worthy, deserving, and whole.

While you might be inclined to put this off or turn the page, possibly because you do not believe you deserve forgiveness, my suggestion is to let the energy of forgiveness make that decision. You're not saying you weren't wrong, but you're allowing yourself to move on. Get out of your head and into your heart. Give forgiveness a chance to enter all the spaces and relationships where love may never have had a chance to fully abide.

In this CLEANSE I highlight the third step, the hum. Before vocalizing it, imagine infusing your hum with the vibration of forgiveness and then let it ripple through your bones, muscles, brain, and even your aura.

Clear Reactivity Begin by taking a deep breath. Now, open your mouth, release your jaw, and let out the longest "aah" you have ever made. Feels great, right? Go ahead, take another big inhale . . . and on the exhale, let out another nice "aah." Pause to notice how you receive the inhale that follows.

Look Inward How I feel in my body right now is . . . inhale through your nose . . . exhale through your nose.

When I resist giving or accepting forgiveness, it makes me feel . . . inhale . . . exhale . . .

Receiving the energy of forgiveness now makes me feel . . . inhale . . . exhale . . .

Loving myself and others now in this way makes me feel . . . inhale . . . exhale . . .

Emit Hum three times.

Activate See it! Imagine releasing any resentments, bitterness, and hurt that you have been holding on to. Perhaps you'll visualize a huge waterfall crashing into a river and becoming the current or maybe a bunch of colorful helium balloons released into the blue sky and drifting ever upward.

Nourish Feel it! Go ahead and stand under that waterfall. Imagine the cleansing water washing over your skin, rinsing all the pain and reactivity away.

Surrender Say: "I allow release. I allow forgiveness. I allow choice. I allow assertiveness. I allow movement."

Ease Say: "I am releasing. I am pure forgiveness. I am clear. I am consciousness. I am energy. I am free."

Cleansing Procrastination

Do you have a pattern of putting things off? Perhaps you live with someone who drags their feet when it comes to getting things done. While some people thrive on waiting until the last minute, others get stuck in the process. In this CLEANSE we will put a little extra love into the first group. I have found that procrastination can often be a sign that you are feeling a little overwhelmed or worried, maybe even frightened. It can also be an indication you are applying a ton of pressure and excessive expectations to yourself. Consider softening a bit, breathe, lower the intensity a couple of notches, and redirect by taking this moment to CLEANSE.

Clear Reactivity Sit or stand up straight with your feet hip-width apart flat on the floor. Tilt your right ear toward your right shoulder. Add a little extra stretch to that movement by extending your right arm straight out to the side, keeping it a little lower than shoulder height. Return your head to center and repeat on the left side. Be sure to move slowly and mindfully when stretching your neck.

Look Inward Getting started on this task now makes me feel . . . inhale through your nose . . . exhale through your nose.

Waiting for others makes me feel . . . inhale through your nose . . . exhale through your nose.

When I am around people who are taking their time without consideration for others, it makes me feel . . . inhale . . . exhale . . .

When I think of where I ought to be and where I am right now, it makes me feel . . . inhale . . . exhale . . .

Acknowledging this pressure makes me feel . . . inhale . . . exhale . . .

Emit Hum three times.

Activate See it! Visualize a scene in nature that reflects movement, such as a flowing stream or a bird in flight.

Nourish Feel it! Imagine the sensation of dipping your hand in the current—the water's temperature and its gentle pressure on your fingertips.

Surrender Say: "I allow movement. I allow action. I allow presence. I allow patience. I allow trust. I allow inner strength."

Ease Say: "I am movement. I am action. I am present. I am patient. I am capable. I am trusting."

Cleansing Impoliteness

Your arms are full of grocery items when someone cuts in front of you in line. *So rude!* Maybe you are waiting to ask a question, buy a ticket, or take a seat on the airplane and the attendant assists the person behind you first. Maybe someone interrupts when you're speaking or ignores you altogether. It is in these moments of impoliteness or lack of consideration you might experience a surge of emotional energy.

You might bite your tongue or express your frustration. While either action will bring awareness to the situation, without a CLEANSE you may carry the rudeness over into the rest of your day. Without emotional processing, these moments can sap your energy, leaving you with a sense of depletion. You may not be able to always control or manage someone else's behavior but what you can do is CLEANSE. The amazing part is the more you CLEANSE the less rattled you become, so if and when you do need to speak up you will do it calmly and with confidence.

Clear Reactivity Squeeze your navel toward your spine as if you were sucking in your stomach as you tighten your belt. Hold it there for three seconds . . . one . . . two . . . three . . . and then release. Repeat two or three more times.

Look Inward How I feel in my body right now is . . . inhale through your nose . . . exhale through your nose.

When someone interrupts me, it makes me feel . . . inhale . . . exhale . . .

When someone cuts in front of me without asking, it makes me feel . . . inhale . . . exhale . . .

Emit Hum three times.

Activate See it! Visualize something calm, patient, tolerant, or harmonious. Perhaps an acorn waiting through winter for spring.

Nourish Feel it! Imagine letting your guard down, the experience of softening your shoulders as you observe the acorn in your hands. Notice how being present to the acorn releases your jaw and relaxes the muscles around your eyes.

Surrender Say: "I allow calm. I allow softening. I allow tolerance. I allow harmony."

Ease Say: "I am calm. I am soft. I am tolerant. I am patient."

Cleansing Rushing

*H*urry up! You are going to be late! Step on it! When we think or hear these things our heart rate accelerates. We may become careless or a little haphazard, driving white-knuckled as we speed down the road or running up the stairs. While you can curb the effects of rushing—things like tension and accidents—by incorporating simple strategies into your life (getting up ten minutes earlier or preparing your breakfast the night before), you might also want to consider throwing in a CLEANSE or two.

Without a CLEANSE, rushing can turn into panic, which can be a challenging state to be in when we need to process an emotion. Not to mention all the minor (and major) accidents that are the result of hurrying. Try to slow down a bit and really notice the last step of this CLEANSE—Ease. Let yourself sink into the quality of energy processed emotions provide. Observe how it can be a vastly distinct experience from the energy of unprocessed emotions.

Clear Reactivity Sit up tall with your feet hip-width apart and curl your toes as if you are making two fists with your feet. This will automatically activate some of your abdominal muscles. Squeeze your toes really hard and hold for a count of one . . . two . . . and then release. Repeat two or three times in a row.

Look Inward How I feel in my body right now is . . . inhale through your nose . . . exhale through your nose.

The idea of slowing down makes me feel . . . inhale . . . exhale . . .

Having this unsettledness inside me now makes me feel . . . inhale . . . exhale . . .

When someone tells me to hurry up, it makes me feel . . . inhale . . . exhale . . .

When I tell myself to hurry up, it makes me feel . . . inhale . . . exhale . . .

Emit Hum three times.

Activate See it! Visualize a scene that is grounding, centered, deliberate, and calm. Perhaps a swan gliding across a pond with purpose, steady and focused. Maybe you are walking barefoot on a beach, mindful of your surroundings yet serene.

Nourish Feel it! Imagine how the sand and water feel underneath your feet. Drop a little deeper into this sensation by relaxing your shoulders.

Surrender Say: "I allow calm. I allow deliberate. I allow centered. I allow steady. I allow grounding. I allow balance."

Ease Say: "I am calm. I am deliberate. I am centered. I am steady. I am grounded. I am balance."

Cleansing for Moodiness

Some call it bitchy, while others call it a bad mood. No matter how you see it, this state of mind can be enough to spoil a good day. Listen, it happens: sometimes you just wake up on the wrong side of the bed, and everything around you irritates you. While it may not seem like such a big deal to you, it keeps the individuals around you on edge. In fact, very often our level of empathy and compassion is determined by mood. When you are in a bad mood, you are less likely to commit kind acts such as holding the door open for someone or giving them a hand with their groceries So often, when I walk people through this CLEANSE, I find that internal pressures begin to surface. Things you are worried about which may be at the forefront of your mind.

Take a moment now and notice what happens to your eyes and mouth when you are in a foul mood. Do you get a pouty look on your face? Do your eyes get smaller? Do you squint? Do your shoulders hunch forward a bit? You don't even have to be in a nasty mood

51

to see how it impacts your appearance and attitude. Move through the Cleanse below and then notice how your facial muscles change. Moodiness can be a sign that you are trying to hold it all together. Regardless of the reason, know the tension you feel in your body is looking for a release.

Clear Reactivity Rub your earlobes with your index fingers and thumbs for about thirty seconds. You will notice right away how your face starts to relax.

Look Inward How I feel in my body right now is . . . inhale through your nose . . . exhale through your nose.

Being in a bad mood makes me feel . . . inhale . . . exhale . . .

Having my mind and body occupied in this way makes me feel . . . inhale . . . exhale . . .

Emit Hum three times.

Activate See it! Visualize an image of happy, content, calm or collected. Perhaps an image of yourself chilling on the beach or relaxing in a hot tub.

Nourish Feel it! Notice the way your muscles soften as you tune into your visualization.

Surrender Say: "I allow softening. I allow release. I allow relief. I allow free."

Ease Say: "I am release. I am calm. I am worthy. I am capable. I am free."

Cleansing Regret

Have you ever experienced a lingering remorse? Have you heard yourself say "If only I hadn't done that" or found yourself wishing for a do-over? If so, it's likely you are holding on to unprocessed regret. When left uncleansed regret can stir up painful feelings of guilt and shame. While some people believe guilt and shame are necessary steps toward change, the Emotional Detox mindset sees it differently. Carrying shame does not foster goodness, however *processing* guilt and shame does. Uncleansed regret can cause you to obsess about what is past, judge, pick apart, and criticize your actions or even your life. Well-being doesn't come from criticism; well-being comes from awareness. While you may not be able to erase or change what you did or did not do, you can revisit the energy around the set of circumstances and avoid future regret by choosing to CLEANSE.

Clear Reactivity Begin by sitting up tall. Fold your right arm across your body and grab the upper part of your left arm at the point between your shoulder and elbow. Then tilt your right ear toward your right shoulder. Use your arm as an anchor to deepen the stretch in your neck a little. Repeat on the left side by grabbing your opposite arm and tilting your left ear toward your left shoulder. Remember to breathe.

Look Inward How I feel in my body right now is . . . inhale through your nose . . . exhale . . . through your nose.

Looking back on some of my choices and decisions makes me feel . . . inhale . . . exhale . . .

When I wish I could have done something differently, it makes me feel . . . inhale . . . exhale . . .

Emit Hum three times.

Activate See it! Visualize a scene filled with contentment, fulfillment, pleasure, or joy. Where would you be? What would you see and sense?

Nourish Feel it! Allow yourself to experience the joy and bliss in your body right now. Even if you have to make it up—whether it is winning the lottery, skipping down a path, or reaching the summit of a mountain—revel in the sensation. Let go of your attachment to a specific image of yourself.

Surrender Say: "I allow bliss. I allow joy. I allow fulfillment. I allow pleasure. I allow release. I allow success."

Ease Say: "I am success. I am free. I am joy. I am pleasure. I am worthy."

Cleansing Intimidation

Intimidation happens when you feel bullied, forced, or pressured. If someone were to raise their voice to a frightening level and shout orders at you—maybe it's your boss, or teacher, or a parent—you might want to run, protect yourself, or fight back, but because of the situation you comply with their demand. Sometimes intimidation can be sensed—maybe you are getting a weird vibe or gut feeling to stay away from someone. In any of these situations, something doesn't feel quite right. Your lack of reaction might even be due to an unconscious memory, a time you felt paralyzed by an extreme sense of threat. I believe some of these reactions are hardwired neurologically and can come from family history—the danger and fear our ancestors once faced. Before you figure out the reason for feeling intimidated, I encourage you to take this moment to CLEANSE to create a healthier foundation that will lead to a nonreactive response.

Clear Reactivity Sit up tall with your feet hip-width apart. Think of your spine as a channel for communication between your gut and brain. Focusing your attention on your lower back, seal off your right nostril with your right thumb and breathe slowly through your left nostril for sixty seconds. Concentrate on inflating your lower back. Keep your breath easy and relaxed.

Look Inward How I feel in my body right now is . . . inhale through your nose . . . exhale through your nose.

When I do not know what to expect or what to do, it makes me feel . . . inhale . . . exhale . . .

Releasing this fear now makes me feel . . . inhale . . . exhale . . .

Emit Hum three times.

Activate See it! Visualize a scene expressing reassurance, calm, safety, and gentleness. Perhaps a butterfly sanctuary.

Nourish Feel it! Imagine a butterfly landing on your hand right now—how gentle and delicate it would be. Notice how your body would need to relax and be present to protect this vulnerable creature.

Surrender Say: "I allow gentle. I allow reassurance. I allow safety. I allow calm. I allow healing."

Ease Say: "I am healing. I am calm. I am safe. I am reassurance. I am free."

Cleansing Powerlessness

Powerlessness happens when you feel you have no control or say in your situation. It might be a drug you can't stop reaching for, a partnership that seems to no longer be working, or the way someone treats you no matter how much you try to make things better or different. It might be a natural disaster or a pandemic. When you succumb to powerlessness it can make you feel deflated, heavy, and depleted. As a result, a part of you may want to fight back and defend yourself, while another part of you may not be up to the task. You see, when a feeling of powerlessness remains uncleansed or unprocessed it can lead to disempowering behaviors like social withdrawal, self-harm, or sabotage. When it comes to an Emotional Detox, you might consider what it means to explore the feeling of surrendering to the events and circumstances over which you have no power—some you may be able to overcome but others are beyond your control. If you are not sure what that means, consider emotional processing as a form of surrender.

57

Clear Reactivity Using the pads of your fingertips, give your scalp a thorough massage by pressing and kneading it as if you were washing your hair. Then move your jaw around a little bit, noticing and breathing into the tingly or sticky sensations.

Look Inward How I feel in my body right now is . . . inhale through your nose . . . exhale through your nose.

When I'm not given any say or agency in a situation, it makes me feel . . . inhale . . . exhale . . .

Having my thoughts, opportunities, or circumstances minimized in this way makes me feel . . . inhale . . . exhale . . .

Having no control makes me feel . . . inhale . . . exhale . . .

Emit Hum three times.

Activate See it! Visualize something that expresses strength, resilience, worthiness, and love, such as an ancient, gigantic tree or the rising sun.

Nourish Feel it! Imagine standing in the shade of the tall tree, touching its sturdy trunk, and looking up at its rustling leaves.

Surrender Say: "I allow expansive. I allow capable. I allow strength. I allow influence. I allow powerful. I allow possibility."

Ease Say: "I am possible. I am strength. I am capable. I am seen. I am heard. I am powerful. I am free."

Cleansing Holding a Grudge

When you think of holding a grudge, you might picture a person holding on to sourness and ranting about a perceived offense years after they were wronged. While that sounds a little dramatic, that is what holding a grudge looks like—you are still bringing up the past. Here is the thing: People generally hold grudges because they harbor unprocessed emotions of bitterness and anger. Rather than allow themselves to process these harsh emotions they cling to them as if they were some sort of life preserver. This is because in a weird way grudges make us feel validated, that we have the right to continue to feel, behave, and think the way we do. For example, let's say you got angry and complained to your neighbor who left their barking dog in the yard all day long. Years after the problem has been resolved, you still ignore the neighbor. Maybe you had every right to complain and maybe the neighbor wasn't as apologetic as they should be, but if you hold on to the story and the negative feelings that surround it for months or years, I am sorry to break it to you, that is holding a grudge. It is not worth hanging onto that stuff! Today is your day to let it go, release, and give yourself permission to heal from any hurt you may be carrying.

Clear Reactivity Cross your arms in front of you—left hand to right shoulder and right hand to left shoulder. Sit up tall with your feet hip-width apart. Drop your chin and swivel your head side to side as you gently stretch your neck. Cross your arms again, this time with the opposite arm on top and repeat the stretch. Pause for one breath.

Look Inward How I feel in my body right now is . . . inhale through your nose . . . exhale through your nose.

Holding on to the past makes me feel . . . inhale . . . exhale . . .

If I allow this reaction to go, it would make me feel . . . inhale . . . exhale . . .

Emit Hum three times.

Activate See it! Visualize an image of fragility, tenderness, vulnerability, and acceptance. Perhaps a slightly cracked vase sitting on the ledge of a shelf.

Nourish Feel it! Imagine your body's reactions as you look at this vase and how quickly you might try to manage the unease. If the discomfort gets too intense, give yourself permission to do one more hum and then move to the next step.

Surrender Say: "I allow vulnerability. I allow imperfection. I allow acceptance. I allow forgiveness. I allow release. I allow fragility. I allow strength. I allow freedom."

Ease Say: "I am strength. I am vulnerability. I am real. I am enough. I am capable. I am valuable. I am free."

Cleansing Sadness

Sadness is a normal, healthy emotion. It makes sense to feel down when we are disappointed or have suffered a loss. When sadness is suppressed over prolonged periods of time it can lead to depression. The antidote to sadness is joy. Not happiness, but *joy*. As I explained in my book *Emotional Detox*, joy and happiness are not the same. Happiness is dependent on circumstances like "I am happy I got a raise" or "I am happy you came to visit." However, joy comes from pure feeling—like the joy of being in the moment. Here is the way I see it: Joy produces happiness. Today, give yourself permission to feel and process past or present sadness. See this as an opportunity to uncover joy.

Clear Reactivity Here you will do an exercise called "smile breath." Sit up tall so your spine is long and lift the corners of your mouth into a smile. Inhale through your nose and let your smile widen as you inflate your abdomen. Hold your smile for one count and then pull your navel toward your spine and release the corners of your mouth on the exhale. Soften your cheeks and repeat the smile breath exercise two or three times.

Look Inward How I feel in my body right now is . . . inhale through your nose . . . exhale through your nose.

When I smile, it makes me feel . . . inhale . . . exhale . . .

Releasing the heaviness in my heart now makes me feel . . . inhale . . . exhale . . .

Emit Hum three times.

Activate See it! Visualize a scene of joy or laughter, such as birds chirping or young children playing together.

Nourish Feel it! Imagine the sensation of hearing the children's laughter, the physical vibrations caused by the giggles.

Surrender Say: "I allow joy. I allow happiness. I allow release. I allow relinquishing. I allow renewal."

Ease Say: "I am renewal. I am joy. I am uplifted. I am smiling. I am happiness. I am free."

Cleansing Poor Self-Esteem

The difference between self-esteem and self-image (which we will get to in the next CLEANSE) is self-esteem is based on how you feel about yourself whereas self-image is how you see or imagine yourself. When it comes to self-esteem, I have found how you feel about yourself is highly influenced by unprocessed emotions. In other words, when you squash, hold back, avoid, or bury your emotions, these actions damage or silence your spirit. Your spirit is the part of you that allows you to trust yourself no matter what. In other words, without spirit there is no belief or faith in anything and as a result you might find yourself feeling down or unhappy with yourself or your situation. This is why poor self-esteem can lead to self-destructive behaviors such as disordered eating or skipping school. Today is about raising energy and shifting some of those emotions you have been suppressing so you can experience a new way of feeling and thinking.

Clear Reactivity Do jumping jacks for about twenty seconds. You can also modify this exercise by sitting up tall in a chair and moving your arms swiftly up and down. The point is to get your heart rate up a little before moving on to the next step.

Look Inward How I am in my body right now is . . . inhale through your nose . . . exhale through your nose.

When I hold back my true sense of who I am, it makes me feel . . . inhale . . . exhale . . .

Disconnecting from my spirit makes me feel . . . inhale . . . exhale . . .

Allowing these feelings to surface now makes me feel . . . inhale . . . exhale . . .

Emit Hum three times.

Activate See it! Visualize something blooming in nature. Perhaps a large tree surrounded by hundreds of flowers.

Nourish Feel it! Imagine sitting under that tree and touching its bark as you smell the flowers.

Surrender Say: "I allow freeing. I allow movement. I allow blossoming. I allow releasing. I allow purging. I allow connection. I allow being."

Ease Say: "I am being. I am releasing. I am movement. I am surrender. I am blooming. I am whole. I am free."

Cleansing Negative Self-Image

Self-image is based on the way you see or envision yourself. How you view your overall appearance, personality, and accomplishments usually in contrast to others. You may see yourself as difficult, unlikable, or boring. Maybe you view yourself as overweight, underweight, unattractive, or old. Self-image starts to develop around age five when we enter "real" school. This is probably when you learned to notice the way people viewed and judged themselves and others. Self-image is highly influenced by society, media, and the types of nurturers and experiences you have had. If you grew up around people with poor self-image or who knocked down your self-image, this might be reflected in you. Very often we criticize ourselves based on what we hear, feel, and observe in others. If you have a poor self-image, it is likely you have been spending quite a bit of time comparing yourself to others, so take a moment and CLEANSE this.

Clear Reactivity Sit up tall and raise your arms over your head. Grab each elbow with the opposite hand. Your forearms will be on the top of your head and you will be framing your face. If you are unable to grab your elbows, you can modify the position by holding on to your wrists. You want to feel a stretch in your armpits and triceps. Once in position, inhale through your mouth for a count of one . . . two . . . three . . . then exhale through your mouth for a count of count of one . . . two . . . three . . . as you pull your navel toward your spine.

Look Inward How I feel in my body right now is . . . inhale through your nose . . . exhale through your nose.

Judging myself in this way makes me feel . . . inhale . . . exhale . . .

Comparing myself to others makes me feel . . . inhale . . . exhale . . .

Having these thoughts and conversations with myself makes me feel . . . inhale . . . exhale . . .

Emit Hum three times.

Activate See it! Visualize what self-acceptance in nature might look like. Perhaps it is floating in a pond or lake that is just the right temperature—not to hot and not too cold.

Nourish Feel it! Imagine resting in the calm, welcoming water as it envelops you like a gentle embrace.

Surrender Say: "I allow uniqueness. I allow self-acceptance. I allow inner beauty. I allow strength. I allow differences."

Ease Say: "I am unique. I am beautiful. I am lovable. I am worthy. I am special."

Cleansing Misdirected Ego

The ego is the fearful part of self. It is the part of you that shows up whenever you are on the cusp of something new, unfamiliar, or different. It is competitive, constricting, and full of doubt. The concept of the ego was formulated by psychoanalyst Sigmund Freud in 1923. He developed it to describe the way your mind can divide itself. Other prominent psychologists later built upon his theory, finding ways to help people cope with these tendencies. While I have great respect for these early pioneers and as an adjunct psychology professor give tribute to them each semester, what I have found is the more you CLEANSE the quieter the voice of the ego gets. In other words, the ego doesn't hold water when it comes to emotions in flow. Similar to a toddler having a tantrum, the more attention you give to the ego the more inflated the ego gets. On the other hand, giving yourself permission to rinse all this reactivity (the ego being a big part of that) provides you with the inner space to discover what life can look and more important feel like as the ego begins to dissolve. If you find it perk up, no problem, just move through this CLEANSE.

Clear Reactivity Take a few seated "sun breaths." To do this, begin by placing your feet flat on the floor. With your arms by your side and your palms turned out, on the inhale raise your hands above your head until your palms touch, then on the exhale lower your hands in prayer position in front of your heart center. Repeat this breathing exercise two or three times in a row.

Look Inward How I feel in my body right now is . . . inhale through your nose . . . exhale through your nose.

Having power and control makes me feel . . . inhale . . . exhale . . .

Not having power and control makes me feel . . . inhale . . . exhale . . .

Now that I no longer feed into those fearful thoughts it makes me feel . . . inhale . . . exhale . . .

Emit Hum three times.

Activate See it! Visualize a scene that represents love, purity, grace, or ease. Recall a moment in your life when you beheld something resourceful or infinite, such as the sun at dawn or the stars on a clear night.

Nourish Feel it! Imagine looking at the sky on a starry night, witnessing the greatness of nature.

Surrender Say: "I allow magnificence. I allow greatness. I allow love. I allow purity. I allow grace."

Ease Say: "I am magnificent. I am humble. I am worthy. I am pure. I am love. I am free."

Cleansing Lack of Purpose

One way suppressed emotions show up is through a feeling of a lack of purpose. If your life seems empty or devoid of meaning, intimacy, and connection it is likely you have heavier emotions such as sadness, grief, and guilt that need to be processed. Without doing so, emotions such as these can siphon the life force out of you, leaving you with a sense of emptiness or hollowness. While it might seem like adults are the only ones who experience lack of purpose, I have also worked with children who do not feel purposeful in their life. This is because our spirit—even at an early age—wants to contribute. In fact, we crave opportunities to bring meaning to this world, yet we can't do this when we are clogged by unprocessed emotions.

Clear Reactivity Allow yourself to consume a meal in silence. Turn off your cell phone, computer, and television. Find a peaceful place, and eat quietly for at least ten minutes. If it's not mealtime, sip a cup of coffee or cool water quietly and intentionally. If you are accustomed to eating in silence, challenge yourself further by putting down your utensils or cup between each bite of food or sip of liquid.

Look Inward How I feel in my body right now is . . . inhale through your nose . . . exhale through your nose.

Sitting quietly makes me feel . . . inhale . . . exhale . . .

Tuning in to the life force, this energy, this breath makes me feel . . . inhale . . . exhale . . .

Connecting to my spirit now makes me feel . . . inhale . . . exhale . . .

Emit Hum three times.

Activate See it! Visualize the energy of a sunset as its colors move through the atmosphere and across the horizon.

Nourish Feel it! Sense the energy from these colors and how they affect the energy inside your body now.

Surrender Say: "I allow inspiration. I allow life. I allow breath. I allow spirit."

Ease Say: "I am spirit. I am breath. I am alive. I am inspired. I am purpose. I am energy. I am free."

Cleansing Feeling Blocked

When emotional reactivity runs at a high level over a long period of time you may find yourself becoming a bit numb or oblivious to what is going on around you. This is because the emotional energy inside your body gets tight, balled up, or congested. One of the ways to recognize blocked energy is if you begin to cut yourself off from the outside world. Perhaps you find yourself withdrawing more, interacting less (avoiding contact), or spending long periods of time on social media.

Blocked energy takes the sparkle out of life. The good news is you can unblock your emotions by tuning in to them, giving them a good CLEANSE, like the one below.

Clear Reactivity Sit up tall with your feet flat on the floor. Rub your palms together vigorously for ten seconds and then place your right hand several inches in front of your throat, keeping your fingers together. Next, slowly circle your palm clockwise as you breathe in and out through your nose for thirty seconds, inflating your abdomen on the inhale, deflating on the exhale.

Look Inward How I feel in my body right now is . . . inhale through your nose . . . exhale through your nose.

When I get sucked into distractions, it makes me feel . . . inhale . . . exhale . . .

Breathing into my body now makes me feel . . . inhale . . . exhale . . .

Untangling myself in this way makes me feel . . . inhale . . . exhale . . .

Emit Hum three times.

Activate See it! Visualize an open window letting a breeze fill the room or perhaps a beautiful ocean.

Nourish Feel it! Imagine you are at the beach right now. Hear the waves, smell the air, and allow the breeze to release you.

Surrender Say: "I allow dissolve. I allow release. I allow open. I allow clear."

Ease Say: "I am clear. I am flow. I am movement. I am fluid. I am free."

Part II

LOVE & RELATIONSHIPS

Relationships often shine a spotlight on the emotions that need to be processed.

The more I share the Emotional Detox and CLEANSE method with people and listen to their fears, the clearer it has become to me that one of our most common fears is losing love. The place this fear shows up the most is through relationships—ironically, the thing we most fear losing. These can be relationships with others as well as the one you have with yourself. This section includes CLEANSEs for both. While you may genuinely believe you have moved on from that horrible breakup, or the older cousin who teased you mercilessly, or that argument with your child, what I have seen time and time again is how these situations harbor emotions like hurt, disappointment, and rejection that can be carried via emotional memories from one relationship to the next unless, of course, you give yourself a moment to process them.

There may be a part of you that is a bit reluctant. Perhaps you feel like you have finally moved on, cleared the air, heck, you may be saying to yourself, "There is no way you are making me revisit those old memories." Let me assure you the CLEANSE is not about revisiting, it is about identifying, releasing, and renewing. Time and time again, I have seen individuals who have undergone years of therapy, moved through the CLEANSE, and were completely blown away at how much better they felt.

There is one more thing—a tip for moving through this section: Try not to justify or explain what you are feeling with your rational mind. Yes, I know you are an adult now and you see things through a different lens, yet when it comes to each CLEANSE, let your body feel what it needs to experience. Remember, it is not about the story as much as it is about an old, familiar, and at times triggering feeling that you are giving permission to be released and resolved. Trust your body and its sensations, trust that breath and spirit are incredibly wise and will be much better at getting to the root of what is happening. When it does you will strengthen not only your relationships with others, but with yourself as well.

Cleansing When You Feel Alone

It is one thing to be alone, yet it is a whole different experience to *feel* alone. Solitude can be a choice or an opportunity. On the other hand, feeling alone can lead to sorrow, frustration, and a sense of abandonment or isolation. While you might believe that you have to be isolated from people to feel alone, that isn't necessarily true. I know people who have been married for years, decades in fact, who carry this unprocessed feeling. One of the things I hear most often when it comes to feeling alone is the idea of being unheard or unsupported. It always amazes me how much hearing and truly listening to others can foster a sense of unity and connection. As you move through this CLEANSE return to the idea of listening to yourself, *really* listening to the statements you are about to repeat.

Clear Reactivity Rub your palms together for about thirty seconds, energizing the heat between them. Place one palm on your forehead and the other over your heart. Breathe in this position for about twenty seconds, acknowledging that you're giving yourself some comfort.

Look Inward How I feel in my body right now is . . . inhale through your nose . . . exhale through your nose.

When I tell myself I can't count on others or I'm better off keeping to myself, it makes me feel . . . inhale . . . exhale . . .

Holding on to these burdens makes me feel . . . inhale . . . exhale . . .

Emit Hum three times.

Activate See it! Visualize a scene of comfort, love, support, strength, and freedom. Perhaps an image of a warm blanket or a cup of tea.

Nourish Feel it! Imagine what that cup of tea would feel like in your hands right now. How it may slow down your racing thoughts, how your shoulders and spine might relax.

Surrender Say: "I allow relaxation. I allow release. I allow support. I allow reliability. I allow trust."

Ease Say: "I am trusting. I am reliability. I am listening. I am heard. I am validated. I am love. I am present. I am free."

Cleansing Fear of Getting Hurt

While writing this book one of my friend's suggested I offer a CLEANSE on trust. At the time she had been dating a man for about a year. I looked at her and said, "Is it really about trust or is it about fear of getting hurt?" She responded with, "Wow. You're right!" When it comes to building trust you have to ask yourself, "What am I afraid of?" It is likely the answer will be pain, abandonment, or getting hurt. Then ask, "How I am I preventing myself from feeling this fear?" One interesting way people do this is by overfocusing on trust and ignoring the underlying feelings. I am not saying trust isn't important, but overfocusing on whether you have it or not could be wreaking havoc on a relationship.

Clear Reactivity Sit up tall with your feet parallel on the floor, hip-width apart, and roll your shoulders back a few times. Set your gaze in a neutral position by focusing on the horizon and holding your chin straight. Notice how when you soften your eyes in this position you are given a gentle yet mindful way to connect to the present moment. Relax your jaw and without judging, observe your breath for thirty to sixty seconds.

Look Inward How I feel in my body right now is . . . inhale through your nose . . . exhale through your nose.

When I overfocus on trust, it makes me feel . . . inhale . . . exhale . . .

Being able to trust makes me feel . . . inhale . . . exhale . . .

Not being able to trust makes me feel . . . inhale . . . exhale . . .

Emit Hum three times.

Activate See it! Visualize a scene of safety, security, love, honesty, and connection. Where would you go in your imagination to feel safe and secure right now? Who might be with you? Perhaps a companion, like a dear friend or your dog.

Nourish Feel it! Notice the sensations inside your body as you become present to this visualization. Do you feel warm, tight, or relaxed? Continue to simply experience without making judgments.

Surrender Say: "I allow love. I allow trust. I allow loyalty. I allow observation. I allow peace. I allow growth."

Ease Say: "I am observant. I am present. I am love. I am trusting. I am faith. I am free."

Cleansing Rejection

Rejection is part of life. We've all faced it at one time or another. There has likely been a time when you have felt excluded, forgotten, or not good enough. Perhaps you didn't make a team, were left off an invitation list, or were ghosted by a friend. Maybe you experienced a bad or sudden breakup. While it seems easy to say "Let it go," the experience of rejection can run deep. In fact, according to psychologist and author Guy Winch in *Psychology Today*, "fMRI studies show that the same areas of the brain become activated when we experience rejection as when we experience physical pain. This is why rejection hurts so much (neurologically speaking)."[1]

If we don't CLEANSE, rejection can feed reactions such as defensiveness, bitterness, sarcasm, self-hatred, and blame. This can weaken your self-esteem, leaving you feeling down in the dumps, severely depressed, or reluctant to try to connect with people in the future. You can see why rejection is an important one to release.

Clear Reactivity Tone your vagus nerve by sitting or standing up tall and letting out a nice, long, audible exhale through your mouth as you scoop your belly inward, gently pulling your navel toward your spine. You can make the sound "aah" and even stick out your tongue, releasing the back of your throat as you do this.

Look Inward How I feel in my body right now is . . . inhale through your nose . . . exhale through your nose.

Now, place your hand over your heart and recite: Carrying this memory in my heart makes me feel . . . inhale . . . exhale . . . .

When I did not feel included, or good enough, it made me feel . . . inhale . . . exhale . . .

Having this be a part of my history makes me feel . . . inhale . . . exhale . . .

Emit Hum three times . . . direct this vibrational medicine toward your heart.

Activate See it! Visualize a scene of renewal, rejuvenation, healing, and strength. Imagine soaking in a hot spring, sitting under an umbrella on the beach, or meditating in a garden.

Nourish Feel it! Notice how you are able to be present to the sounds and sensations around you.

Surrender Say: "I allow healing. I allow rejuvenation. I allow strength. I allow wholeness. I allow inclusion. I allow belonging. I allow nourishment."

Ease Say: "I am belonging. I am nourishment. I am strength. I am enough. I am free."

Cleansing Conflict Around Money

Money is a topic that comes up often in relationships. Without cleansing, individuals can easily fall into patterns of reactivity. Rather than process their fear around losing money or not having enough, instead individuals may resort to behaviors such as complaining, judging, comparing and contrasting (e.g., who makes more, spends more), which of course only makes things worse. I have also seen couples keep their spending under the radar (e.g., pay in cash or hide a receipt) as a way to "keep the peace" in the home. I too have been there; my husband always jokes with me, tells me when it comes to letting him know how much something cost, I suddenly get a case of amnesia (*um, hum, around, ish*). I always say, if you want more money, CLEANSE what is showing up in your relationships. Money flows better when you are not wasting your precious energy covering up, arguing, or hiding your true feelings.

Clear Reactivity Sit up tall and place one hand on your heart. Inhale through your nose. Close your eyes and make an "mmm" sound with your mouth closed as you extend your exhale. Notice the vibration you create in your chest, torso, and lower abdomen when you emit this sound. Repeat this two or three times.

Look Inward How I feel in my body right now is . . . inhale through your nose . . . exhale through your nose.

When the bills, spending, costs get out of control, it makes me feel. . . . inhale . . . exhale . . .

And when my partner (child, sibling) asks me for money, it makes me feel . . . inhale . . . exhale . . .

Being stressed out over money makes me feel . . . inhale . . . exhale . . .

Emit Hum three times.

Activate See it! Visualize a scene of calm, abundant and flowing. What shows up in your mind's eye for you today? Rows of flowers, plentiful fruit on a tree.

Nourish Feel it! Imagine being in this space right now, receiving all the energy it has to offer.

Surrender Say: "I allow calm. I allow flow. I allow mindfulness. I allow consciousness. I allow freedom."

Ease Say: "I am comfort. I am mindful. I am honest, I am clarity. I am flow. I am relief. I am free."

Cleansing Judgment

Do you find yourself judging the actions of people around you and finding fault? Maybe you are having a challenging time figuring out how to fit into a group and judging yourself? Or perhaps you feel judged by your partner and you feel they look at you in a critical way. Maybe you feel like the people in your life do not recognize the good in you or view you as lazy, uptight, or selfish. In some cases having a bit of discerning judgment can be a good thing especially if you are in a situation that may not be safe or healthy. However, if the feeling you are experiencing is chronic and it comes up more often than not, then you have something to CLEANSE. Here is the thing, you can't judge and heal at the same time. It just doesn't work that way, so replace the judgment with the CLEANSE.

Clear Reactivity Sit up tall and place your tongue behind your two front teeth on the roof of your mouth. This will open up the airway in your throat. Holding your tongue in this position, begin to inhale through your nose, inflating your abdomen, and exhale through your nose, pulling your navel in, for about thirty to sixty seconds.

Look Inward How I feel in my body right now is . . . inhale through your nose . . . exhale through your nose.

Focusing on my thoughts in this way makes me feel . . . inhale . . . exhale . . .

Having these thoughts now makes me feel . . . inhale . . . exhale . . .

Emit Hum three times.

Activate See it! Visualize a scene of acceptance, openness, love, kindness, and wisdom. Perhaps an ancient, sacred space such as a church, temple, sanctuary, or garden.

Nourish Feel it! Imagine being in that space now. You may find yourself in tune with and appreciative of what is around you.

Surrender Say: "I allow presence. I allow love. I allow understanding. I allow wisdom. I allow teaching. I allow learning. I allow calm."

Ease Say: "I am learning. I am calm. I am present. I am acceptance. I am appreciation. I am free."

Cleansing Jealousy

Jealousy is a complex emotion that often contains undigested shame, insecurity, anger, and abandonment. Perhaps this is why when left unprocessed it can drive people to do callous and hurtful things. Jealousy is often spiked with envy and hateful thinking. As much as it can be difficult to admit these types of feelings, we have all had them at one point or another. Even people who are in committed loving relationships can find themselves dealing with jealousy and envy.

With that said, not everyone experiences jealousy at the same intensity. It will depend on your history and your unconscious and conscious memories of childhood. If you experienced deep rejection or feelings of mental or physical abandonment as a child, jealousy may be one of your unprocessed emotions. Jealousy may arise in both conscious ways (like when you feel like someone is getting undeserved attention) and unconscious ways (like when you make a snarky comment about someone after a few cocktails), but no matter how it shows up, it is an indication that you need to revisit this CLEANSE.

Clear Reactivity Raise your arms above your head, interlace your fingers, and twist your wrists so the palms of your hands are facing the ceiling. This will feel like a big stretch. Relax your shoulders and consciously bend at the waist from one side to the other. Then release the position, and inhale . . . and exhale . . . naturally. Repeat the entire sequence two or three times in a row.

Look Inward How I feel in my body right now is . . . inhale through your nose . . . exhale through your nose.

When I compare myself or my situation to others, it makes me feel . . . inhale . . . exhale . . .

When I see someone else doing well, being praised, or valued by others, it makes me feel . . . inhale . . . exhale . . .

Emit Hum three times. Be sure to do this slowly, pausing to receive a full breath before beginning the next round.

Activate See it! Visualize where you would feel welcome and safe. Perhaps a farm kitchen with muffins or pie baking in the oven.

Nourish Feel it! Imagine walking into that kitchen. Is it warm and accepting? Does it have the fresh scent of homemade blueberry muffins? Breathe that in now.

Surrender Say: "I allow special. I allow comfort. I allow presence. I allow healing. I allow inner peace."

Ease Say: "I am accepted. I am love. I am present. I am alive. I am healing. I am at peace."

Cleansing Secrets

Have you ever felt like someone was talking behind your back or keeping you out of the loop on purpose? Have you ever felt like someone wasn't telling you the whole truth? Or maybe you have something you might be hiding from someone. You have knowledge or details about something but choose to keep it quiet, so you do not cause any "problems." If you are familiar with twelve-step programs such as Alcoholics Anonymous you may be familiar with the phrase "You are only as sick as your secrets." What I have learned is secrets contaminate your energy in a way similar to how smoke might pollute the air you breathe. You can still breathe but it is not as healthy for you to take it in. Left covered up or buried, over time secrets may not reveal themselves through words or actions but can surface through reactivity and triggers. When we CLEANSE secrets we allow them to release, and as this occurs growth and healing are permitted to happen.

Clear Reactivity Hum a tune (like "Happy Birthday"). This will help lift your energy.

Look Inward How I feel in my body right now is . . . inhale through your nose . . . exhale through your nose.

Keeping this secret inside me makes me feel . . . inhale . . . exhale . . .

When I sense others may be talking behind my back, it makes me feel . . . inhale . . . exhale . . .

And when I sense someone is being dishonest with me, it makes me feel. . . . inhale . . . exhale . . .

Emit Hum three times.

Activate See it! Visualize someplace that is pure, honest, open, or vulnerable. Perhaps an open field with intense winds or a clear stream.

Nourish Feel it! Imagine dipping your feet in that pure water. Does it feel cool and refreshing?

Surrender Say: "I allow open. I allow transparency. I allow honest. I allow pure. I allow clean. I allow growth. I allow freedom."

Ease Say: "I am open. I am transparent. I am pure. I am honest. I am growth. I am surrender. I am free."

Cleansing
Deflection

Deflection is something you see quite often in relationships. For example, one person might begin talking about something and want to seek a resolution but the other diverts the conversation to an entirely different subject. Or think about those couples that spend the majority of their dates meeting up with other couples and friends so they do not have to face or deal with some of the raw stuff (feelings) that may be coming up in their relationships. The challenge with deflection is eventually your loved ones or friends might notice how you use it and begin to sense your ambivalence about taking a conversation or relationship any deeper. As a result, people in your life may learn to avoid or tread lightly around certain topics. When deflection becomes a way to manage your emotions without awareness it can begin to place invisible barriers around you. This sends a message to others; they can only get so close or go so far. While in some cases deflection can be a heathy way to put into place some boundaries and limitations, it is important you notice when and if it interferes with your emotional intimacy and connection. I say when in doubt, choose to CLEANSE.

Clear Reactivity Begin this breathing exercise by opening your mouth fairly wide and inhaling slowly, concentrating on inflating your abdomen. Then exhale with a short and slightly sharper breath by pulling your navel toward your spine. You may even hear yourself make an audible "ha" sound when you do so. Repeat the whole thing two or three times. Pause before moving to the next step.

Look Inward How I feel in my body right now is . . . inhale through your nose . . . exhale through your nose.

When I distract myself and others from what is coming up for me, it makes me feel . . . inhale . . . exhale . . .

The thought of dealing with my emotions makes me feel . . . inhale . . . exhale . . .

Certain emotions, confrontations, and conversations make me feel . . . inhale . . . exhale . . .

Emit Hum three times.

Activate See it! Visualize a scene involving focus and concentration. Perhaps you are taking a close-up picture of a flower, such as a rose.

Nourish Feel it! Imagine smelling the fragrance of this rose as you focus your camera lens to zoom in on the tiny patterns in the petals.

Surrender Say: "I allow focus. I allow direct. I allow open. I allow release. I allow harmony."

Ease Say: "I am focus. I am direct. I am straightforward. I am calm. I am harmony."

Cleansing Blame

Blame is when you assign wrong or being bad to either yourself or someone else. When you are in the reactive state of blame, it is like saying "Whatever happened is because of *you*! It's your fault I feel and behave this way." When it comes to relationships, blame can sound like "You always leave when things get tough" or "If you didn't act this way this would not have happened." Think of blame as a fault-finder, it tends to be critical, close-minded, and judgmental in nature.

On the other hand, you might be quick to blame yourself. Do you often feel accountable for other people's actions? Do you blame yourself for things that are out of your control? Are you quick to throw yourself under the bus? Do you say "I'm sorry" a lot? Perhaps you apologize profusely for other people's behaviors or your own or find yourself managing your emotions and those of the people around you by making it all your fault even when it isn't. If this is you, then dear one, you are tossing your power away. You are basically saying, "Universe, I am not done with this dynamic or pattern so keep showing me situations where I feel powerless." By choosing to CLEANSE today, you are choosing to take your power back.

Clear Reactivity Using your peace fingers, massage the area behind your earlobes for about thirty seconds. Notice how your body expands and you start to take deeper, fuller breaths.

Look Inward How I feel in my body right now is . . . inhale through your nose . . . exhale through your nose.

Being judged or criticized makes me feel . . . inhale . . . exhale . . .

When I accuse or find fault, it makes me feel . . . inhale . . . exhale . . .

When I tell myself it must be my fault, it makes me feel . . . inhale . . . exhale . . .

Emit Hum three times.

Activate See it! Visualize something that is grounding and straightforward. Perhaps a fragrant cup of coffee in the morning or a ripe orange hanging from a branch."

Nourish Feel it! Imagine picking the orange off the tree and peeling it, smelling the fragrance of the ripe fruit.

Surrender Say: "I allow praise. I allow appreciation. I allow grounding. I allow freedom."

Ease Say: "I am appreciation. I am whole. I am pure. I am receiving. I am love."

Cleansing Defensiveness

Defensiveness happens when you feel like you are under attack. Perhaps you feel like someone is putting you down or crossing the line. As a result you may find yourself quick to defend yourself with statements such as, "I do everything around here" or "No matter what I do it is never enough." In relationships, defensiveness can be recognized by the use of "you" as in "You always" or "You never . . ."

If we do not CLEANSE defensiveness we can feel a bit touchy, cold, or aloof. You may find yourself giving someone the cold shoulder, limiting eye contact, or distancing yourself from others. Defensiveness can also show up internally, perhaps by feeling personally attacked by your community, the news, or a social media interaction. Perhaps you are feeling the need to protect your belief systems, values, and culture. Think of a CLEANSE as one of your greatest forms of protection. It releases subconscious and conscious emotions, allowing you to vibrate at a higher energetic frequency and to experience more love, calm, and security.

Clear Reactivity Begin by sitting or standing up tall, chin pointing to the earth. Use your peace-sign fingers to gently press into your abdomen about an inch above your navel. Move your fingers an inch away from your navel and do one more press. Move your fingers sideways in the other direction and press. Repeat this three times in a row: press, move your fingers over an inch, press, move over another inch, and press. Take a breath . . . inhale . . . exhale.

Look Inward How I feel in my body right now is . . . inhale through your nose . . . exhale through your nose.

When I am on the defensive, it makes me feel . . . inhale . . . exhale . . .

When I have to protect myself or others, it makes me feel . . . inhale . . . exhale . . .

Emit Hum three times.

Activate See it! Visualize openness, safety, calm, serene, and peaceful.

Nourish Feel it! Imagine a cat or a dog rolling playfully in the dirt, or waves gently brushing the sand.

Surrender Say: "I allow safety. I allow security. I allow respect. I allow calm. I allow ease."

Ease Say: "I am open. I am thriving. I am space. I am safe. I am respect. I am free."

Cleansing Negativity

Negativity can show up as feeling a little grumpy, irritated, or moody. We can all wake up on the wrong side of the bed sometimes, but when this state of glumness begins to interfere with your ability to connect with yourself and others, when the dark moods overwhelm the light, this is when you know you could benefit from a CLEANSE.

Other ways to recognize negativity are through behaviors such as personal jabs, sarcasm, or picking on someone and then telling them you were only joking. Or when you find yourself quick to dismiss possibilities for yourself or others—an absence of optimism. Think of negativity as being like a heavy fog. Energetically it can feel like a weight or a thickness overwhelming you. Without a CLEANSE, this pressure compresses your emotions, skewing your perception into black or white, good or bad, right or wrong thinking leaving no room for nuance or hope. When you feel that way a CLEANSE will help clear the fog and shine light on your mood, so you can begin to connect to others from your true nature: love.

Clear Reactivity Begin by listening to some calming music. Choose something soothing yet upbeat. (When I searched for "calming upbeat music" on Google I found a lot of options.) Keep the music playing in the background as you stretch your neck from left to right holding for a count of one . . . two . . . three . . . on each side. Feel free to keep this music on for your entire CLEANSE.

Look Inward How I feel in my body right now is . . . inhale through your nose . . . exhale through your nose.

Listening to this upbeat music makes me feel . . . inhale . . . exhale . . .

When this heaviness is around me, it makes me feel . . . inhale . . . exhale . . .

Feeling the beat of this music now makes me feel . . . inhale . . . exhale . . .

Emit Hum three times.

Activate See it! Visualize something positive, blissful, and fun. Perhaps diving into a pool on a scorching summer day.

Nourish Feel it! Imagine letting loose, splashing in the water, and giving in to heartwarming laughter.

Surrender Say: "I allow fun. I allow loose. I allow freedom. I allow joy. I allow bliss."

Ease Say: "I am joy. I am fun. I am loose. I am free. I am bliss."

Cleansing
Withdrawing

Withdrawing is when you remove yourself from a situation so you can manage or avoid the emotions that may be surfacing inside you. While removing yourself to calm down can be a good thing, when it goes on too long or it becomes a way you escape or avoid processing your emotions it can be isolating and can contribute to an atmosphere of fear and insecurity. Since we are directing each CLEANSE in this section toward relationships, know that withdrawal behaviors can trigger feelings of rejection, hurt, and unworthiness in the people around us. In other words, they may feel you care more about something other than them—work, the gym, watching television, or even an addictive behavior—than you care about your relationship with them.

Here is the thing: When used as a way to avoid emotions that need to be processed, withdrawal behaviors generally make everyone feel unsafe and uncertain. This CLEANSE and processing the emotions you're withdrawing from can be the first step toward reconnection.

Clear Reactivity Raise your arms over your head, interlace your fingers, turn your palms up, and give yourself a nice big stretch. Really release and open up your armpits; this will help loosen your jaw. Drop your arms to your sides, tilt your head to the left and roll your neck in a half circle, then do the same on the right side. Repeat this two or three times in a row. Finally, sit up tall and observe your breath for a count of one . . . two . . . three . . . four . . . five . . . allowing yourself to exhale fully on the final count.

Look Inward How I feel in my body right now is . . . inhale through your nose . . . exhale through your nose.

When I close myself off, it makes me feel . . . inhale . . . exhale . . .

Shutting down my emotions, it makes me feel . . . inhale . . . exhale . . .

When others close themselves off to me, it makes me feel . . . inhale . . . exhale . . .

Emit Hum three times.

Activate See it! Visualize the experience of connection, engagement, or presence. Where would you go to stimulate this feeling? Perhaps a place you would go to hear live music.

Nourish Feel it! Imagine remaining in a state of presence today. How would your body react as you hold your attention on the moment? Would your shoulders begin to soften and relax? What about your toes?

Surrender Say: "I allow engagement. I allow progress. I allow presence. I allow discomfort. I allow movement. I allow release."

Ease Say: "I am present. I am here. I am now. I am progress. I am at peace."

Cleansing Abandonment

I f we don't do a CLEANSE, abandonment can feel like you have a gaping hole in your heart. If you have ever had someone break up with you or leave you with little explanation, then it is likely you have experienced what this feels like. Some people report it as a similar feeling to betrayal, while others share that it's more like feeling unsupported or ignored. Sometimes the person who abandons you can't help it—they've died or been forced to move far away because of work or family obligations.

Whether it is a crisis, something smaller but still hurtful like a family member unfriending you on social media, or someone who just seems to have vanished from your life without resolution or explanation, what shows up when this emotion is unprocessed can easily seep into other areas of your life. As a result, you may find yourself struggling from fatigue or exhaustion or a resistance to making new friendships or romantic connections.

Even if you have not experienced abandonment yourself it is likely you have been or currently are around someone who has. A parent, partner, or child may be struggling with the grief and sense of disconnection abandonment can bring. Since we are all interconnected on an emotional and spiritual level, a CLEANSE can be a loving way to serve yourself and others.

Clear Reactivity Stand up tall with your feet together. Raise your arms overhead and interlace your fingers. Bend at the waist to one side (like a crescent moon) and then to the other. Repeat this routine two or three times. Now, drop your arms by your sides, inhale through your nose for a count of one . . . two . . . three . . . and exhale through your nose for a count of one . . . two . . . three . . . as you pull your navel toward your spine.

Look Inward How I feel in my body right now is . . . inhale through your nose . . . exhale through your nose.

Sensing this energy inside me now makes me feel . . . inhale . . . exhale . . .

When my **energy** gets low or absent, it makes me feel . . . inhale . . . exhale . . .

And I cope with feeling this by . . . inhale . . . exhale . . .

Emit Hum three times.

Activate See it! Visualize erasing—from a chalkboard or a computer screen—all the stories and narratives preserving the feeling of abandonment that no longer serves you, perhaps the way an ocean tide sweeps the shells and rocks from a beach or a hard rain rinses the pollen from the air.

Nourish Feel it! Imagine sinking your toes in the sand or standing in the pouring rain, allowing yourself to become soaked and purified.

Surrender Say: "I allow energy. I allow openness. I allow validation. I allow approval. I allow completion."

Ease Say: "I am energy. I am open. I am validation. I am love. I am belonging. I am free."

Cleansing Disconnection

It is normal and healthy for relationships to fluctuate between states of feeling completely connected and disconnected. These shifts in balance happen to everyone, but when a relationship is more heavily weighted in disconnection this can lead to tension, stress, and arguments. Maybe you feel like your partner or your child never pays attention to the things you say, or even when they do, they don't really care how you feel and so you bicker. The unfortunate part is, without awareness these disagreements can turn to harsh criticism, put-downs, and serious misunderstandings. This can make it difficult for you to function in other areas of your life such as concentrating at work or tending to your own needs. If you are having difficulty getting along with others or feel like someone you were once connected to has broken the link between you, take some time today to CLEANSE.

Clear Reactivity If the weather permits, spend a few minutes sitting in the sun. If the sun is not out, take a moment to imagine it shining on you.

Look Inward How I feel in my body right now is . . . inhale through your nose . . . exhale through your nose.

When I am disconnected from someone, it makes me feel . . . inhale . . . exhale . . .

When we are not in sync, it makes me feel . . . inhale . . . exhale . . .

Being ignored makes me feel . . . inhale . . . exhale . . .

Emit Hum three times.

Activate See it! Visualize an image of warmth, comfort, love, and connection. Perhaps sitting in a lounge chair on a sunny day.

Nourish Feel it! Imagine the warmth from the sun's rays. Notice if it helps you feel more relaxed and present.

Surrender Say: "I allow safety. I allow warmth. I allow connection. I allow love."

Ease Say: "I am love. I am connected. I am thriving. I am free."

Cleansing Distrust

Have you ever had that feeling inside your stomach when something didn't feel or sound right? Perhaps you are hearing another person's side of a story, and you are starting to pick up on all the little inconsistencies. Or maybe you are noticing a pattern, perhaps you are basing what you feel on past experiences, that whatever is said or done in the moment won't last. Here is the way I see trust: It is so essential yet at the same time so overrated. You need trust so that you can build a solid foundation between people, yet if you overfocus on not having it or losing it, you can really make a mountain out of a molehill. However, if someone squeaks out a white lie, or says something they don't remember because they were so wrapped up in the heat (stress) of the moment, you may not want to throw your whole day off over that one. Now, I am certainly not promoting white lies, but what I am saying is people react when they feel attacked, disrespected, or hurt. It is just a reality; however, it doesn't necessarily mean they are a bad person or you can't trust them. Let's CLEANSE.

Clear Reactivity Sit up tall with your feet parallel, hip-width apart. Turn your head and gently gaze over your right shoulder for three seconds, then return to center. Repeat on the left side.

Look Inward How I feel in my body right now is . . . inhale through your nose . . . exhale through your nose.

When something doesn't feel right, it makes me feel . . . inhale . . . exhale . . .

When I have these feelings, it reminds me of a time I felt . . . inhale . . . exhale . . .

Experiencing this feeling inside my body now makes me feel . . . inhale . . . exhale . . .

Emit Hum three times.

Activate See it! Visualize a scene of safety, calm, love, trust, and sincerity. Perhaps an image of someone holding your hand and helping you up a hill.

Nourish Feel it! Imagine gripping a solid hand, allowing the strength of the support to pull you up.

Surrender Say: "I allow calm. I allow trust. I allow discernment. I allow healing. I allow new beginnings."

Ease Say: "I am trust. I am discernment. I am truth. I am happiness. I am enough. I am free."

Cleansing After an Argument

So you had an argument. *Ugh*—the feeling after sharp words, looks, and comments are exchanged. I know I've been there. In the heat of the moment you might feel like "Finally I can get this shit off my chest," but then later when you are alone or the dust has settled those horrible feelings of regret, fear, anger, sadness, doubt, and frustration can set in. While there is nothing like a genuine apology to help heal the wounds, offering a CLEANSE to the feelings coming up will also help and may even help you make that apology. Look at it this way, it is not just about the argument, clearly there was something building up inside of you that led you to that place. So rather than berate yourself, learn from the experience as you take time to CLEANSE what is showing up. Remember, very often the emotions you carry go far deeper than you may realize.

Clear Reactivity Bring your left arm over your head as you sit up tall. Bend your arm at the elbow as your fingers touch your neck. It will feel like a triceps stretch. Hold for three to five seconds. Then do this again with your right arm, reaching above your head, bending at the elbow, and stretching your triceps. Then tilt your head side to side, right ear to right shoulder, left ear toward left shoulder, and bring your head back to center, hands on your lap as you observe your breathing.

Look Inward How I feel in my body right now is . . . inhale through your nose . . . exhale through your nose.

When I lose my cool or say things I do not mean it makes me feel . . . inhale . . . exhale . . .

Holding these sensations and situations inside makes me feel . . . inhale . . . exhale . . .

When things escalate or get heated I feel . . . inhale . . . exhale . . .

Emit Hum three times.

Activate See it! Visualize an image of loosening, perhaps leaves on a tree gently blowing in the wind, unzipping your coat, or taking off your shoes.

Nourish Feel it! Imagine what it feels like to remove a tight pair of shoes, spread your toes in the warm sand.

Surrender Say: "I allow calm. I allow release. I allow open. I allow breath. I allow peace."

Ease Say: "I am calm. I am quiet. I am breath. I am at peace."

Cleansing Enabling

Enabling happens when you do things for others that they are very capable of doing themselves. Often, they would even benefit from doing these things for themselves. For example, you may be washing your adult child's laundry, making appointments for other people, or cleaning up messes that aren't yours. Enabling can also show up in other ways, such as making excuses for someone's addictive or unkind behavior, or protecting your loved one by covering up for them when they've made a mistake. It can be taking on someone's responsibilities and even their emotions. Emotional Detoxes allow us to recognize how we may be preventing someone else from feeling their emotions as a way to control or manage our own. The reality is when we interfere with someone else feeling their own emotions we inevitably stifle their ability to mature and grow. This is likely because we subconsciously tell ourselves that for some reason it is our responsibility to be accountable for someone else's pain. Remember, when it comes to an Emotional Detox, feeling does not cause pain, resisting feeling does. A CLEANSE will release this pattern.

Clear Reactivity Sit up tall, feet hip-width apart. Bring your arms overhead as you inhale through your nose. On the exhale, let out an audible, "ha" sound as you lower your arms. Repeat this sequence three more times, and lengthen your "haaaa" on each exhale. Breathe.

Look Inward How I feel in my body right now is . . . inhale through your nose . . . exhale through your nose.

Letting others move through their own emotions makes me feel . . . inhale . . . exhale . . .

When I try to take over or rescue others, it makes me feel . . . inhale . . . exhale . . .

Taking a step back and breathing into what is showing up inside of me now makes me feel . . . inhale . . . exhale . . .

Emit Hum three times.

Activate See it! Visualize an image of growth, confidence, strength, and stability. Perhaps a beautiful strong tree that has survived the harshest storms.

Nourish Feel it! Imagine what it would feel like to have inner confidence, unwavering trust, growth, and stability.

Surrender Say: "I allow resiliency. I allow strength. I allow trust. I allow confidence. I allow surrender."

Ease Say: "I am growth. I am strength. I am relinquishing. I am trusting. I am free."

Cleansing
Infidelity

Infidelity happens when one or both parties break a bond of trust. Usually we think of this in terms of adultery, which can be emotional, physical, sexual, or a combination of the above. Infidelity can be defined as lying in a relationship, cheating, or fooling around. Whether you have engaged in adultery, witnessed it as a child, or had a partner who was unfaithful, these types of situations can leave traces of bitterness, resentment, hurt, shame, and unworthiness. I have seen people cope with infidelity by avoiding bringing up the past, using repercussions for past behavior as a threat, or suffering in silence. While the experience of infidelity can be tremendously heartbreaking, it can also be a source of renewal, strength, and growth—either back together or apart. The key is to process rather than restrain yourself from experiencing emotional flow.

Clear Reactivity For this one I would like you to lie down on your back. Put your head on a pillow. Place one hand on your heart and one hand on your lower abdomen. Close your eyes and mouth and breathe into the space that reaches from your lower belly to your heart center. Feel the rise or inflation of your abdomen on the inhale and deflation as you press your navel to spine on the exhale. Notice if lying on your back deepens or shifts your breath.

Look Inward How I feel in my body right now is . . . inhale through your nose . . . exhale through your nose.

Losing my sense of self in our relationship in this way made me feel . . . inhale . . . exhale . . .

When I found out I was betrayed, it made me feel . . . inhale . . . exhale . . .

Giving myself the opportunity to release this now makes me feel . . . inhale . . . exhale . . .

Emit Hum three times.

Activate See it! Visualize an image of something faithful, dependable, honest, fair, and open. Perhaps a river that never runs dry or a statue of a spiritual figure who inspires you.

Nourish Feel it! Imagine touching the water of this river, letting it flow through your fingers as you close your eyes and breathe. Trust in this unwavering presence in your life.

Surrender Say: "I allow flow. I allow trust. I allow transparency. I allow forgiveness. I allow a breakthrough. I allow breaking free."

Ease Say: "I am learning. I am growth. I am infinite. I am healing. I am enough. I am love. I am free."

Cleansing Your Relationship with Your Children

B roken relationships can be so difficult and weigh on you in more ways than you might realize. While you or your child might seem like they moved on from a misunderstanding or a larger conflict, cleansing what was or what is can be an important part of the healing journey. If there is broken trust, tension, or conflict between you and your child recognize that a genuine apology can help. Or maybe you and your child have a tendency to butt heads; you love each other to pieces, yet your personalities tend to clash. Trust the CLEANSE to help ease some of that tension while allowing you to release the past and focus on the now. As this occurs you will begin to take things less personally, gain a sense of compassion toward yourself and your child, and probably do a better job being a parent instead of a combatant.

When blended with a consistent choice of actions like being fully present, your relationship has the opportunity to thrive in unimaginable ways.

Clear Reactivity Take off your shoes and socks and gently massage the soles of your feet. You can use a cream, oil, or just squeeze your foot by pressing the pads of your fingers into the areas that feel tight or tender. Be sure to switch feet. Do this for one minute per foot before you proceed to step two.

Look Inward How I feel in my body right now is . . . inhale through your nose . . . exhale through your nose.

Healing this relationship makes me feel . . . inhale . . . exhale . . .

Uncovering the unconscious wedges between us now makes me feel . . . inhale . . . exhale . . .

Not healing this relationship makes me feel . . . inhale . . . exhale . . .

When things do not feel right between us, it makes me feel . . . inhale . . . exhale . . .

Emit Hum three times.

Activate See it! Visualize an image that is soothing, one that evokes gratitude and pleasure. Where would you go to experience and express gratitude? Perhaps a water fountain in a garden or a park bench.

Nourish Feel it! Imagine feeling gratitude for the love or kindness of another, how that might nourish and expand your heart. See yourself receiving and giving a warm hug.

Surrender Say: "I allow expansion. I allow warmth. I allow growth. I allow discomfort. I allow ease. I allow faith."

Ease Say: "I am expansion. I am growth. I am understanding. I am comfort. I am discomfort. I am enough."

Cleansing Your Relationship with Other Family Members

Do you have some unresolved issues or broken connections with other family members? A sibling, cousin, aunt, or stepfather? Maybe your parents? Or perhaps you just can't stand who your brother married. Or the way your mother-in-law treats your kids. Ask yourself, how have your feelings around this affected your other relationships? Do you find yourself avoiding family gatherings? Or maybe you just go along with things despite what you are truly feeling. What emotions around the situation might you be burying? When it comes to family, it can truly bring out the worse or best in others. Things like divorce, a death, money, abuse, and even political disagreements can be difficult to get through and get over. When left uncleansed, even a simple disagreement can cause friction that can linger for years. Think of this CLEANSE as an opportunity to release some of the tight, constricted, stored-up energy, creating a deeper sense of unity and connection.

Clear Reactivity Sit up nice and tall in a chair with both feet flat on the floor, hip-width apart. Rub the palms of your hands together in front of you for about ten seconds. Then take your right hand, and with your palm facing inward, hold it about eight inches from your chest in front of your heart center. Close your fingers and gently make a small clockwise circle over your chest with your right hand. Do this about five times until you feel your jaw release and your breathing become a little deeper.

Look Inward How I feel in my body right now is . . . inhale through your nose . . . exhale through your nose.

When I allow myself to think, feel, and tune in to this family member, it makes me feel . . . inhale . . . exhale . . . (If the discomfort gets intense here, put your hand back in front of your heart and circulate the energy again to support the process.)

Releasing these thoughts and reactions now makes me feel . . . inhale . . . exhale . . .

Emit Hum three times.

Activate See it! Visualize an image of peace, serenity, self-awareness, calm, and ease. Perhaps an image of a feather floating in the air or calm ocean waves.

Nourish Feel it! Imagine how it would feel to touch that feather, how still and present your body would be. Breathe into that presence now.

Surrender Say: "I allow release. I allow peace. I allow serenity. I allow calm. I allow stillness."

Ease Say: "I am still. I am aware. I am consciousness. I am relief. I am free."

Cleansing Diminishment

Sometimes in a relationship you might feel like you do not have a say, you're made to feel small—minimized or diminished. Perhaps you even feel like you are being pushed or bossed around. I once worked with a married couple and the husband said to me, "I call her 'master.' She tells me what to do and I pretty much do it." While some couples can be lighthearted about these dynamics, others find themselves feeling frustrated and powerless. If you feel like you are having a challenging time voicing your opinion or you feel like you are being treated like you are a child, this CLEANSE is for you. While in many cases, these feelings stem from suppressed childhood emotions being brought to your attention by the relationship you are in now, think of this as opportunity to release the underpinning of what is really happening. Is there a part of you that feels guilty, like you are doing something wrong if you don't do as you are told? Let's CLEANSE.

Clear Reactivity With your palms turned upward, make your hands into a fist, keeping your thumbs on the outside touching the middle joint of your ring finger. Turn your palms over and place your hands in your lap in this position. Breathe in and out through your nose for twenty seconds.

Look Inward How I feel in my body right now is . . . inhale through your nose . . . exhale through your nose.

Having someone speak to me in that way makes me feel . . . inhale . . . exhale . . .

When I feel like I do not have a choice, it makes me feel . . . inhale . . . exhale . . .

Being told what to do makes me feel . . . inhale . . . exhale . . .

Emit Hum three times.

Activate See it! Visualize an image of innocence, purity, and wholeness. Maybe a newborn lamb or a cooing baby.

Nourish Feel it! Imagine being around this energy. How do you feel in your body now? Soft, calm, peaceful?

Surrender Say: "I allow purity. I allow innocence. I allow calm. I allow freedom. I allow wholeness."

Ease Say: "I am pure. I am innocent. I am lovable. I am nurtured. I am calm. I am free. I am whole."

Cleansing When You Miss Your Significant Other

To miss someone is to long for their presence. Are you in or have you been in a long-distance relationship? Maybe your significant other is in the military, travels for their company, or works long hours. Maybe you miss the way you used to be as a couple and the way you would connect when you were together. If so, this CLEANSE will help you release the emotions you may be pushing away to cope with your situation. You might overcompensate and become clingy, fearful, or distrustful.

When emotions related to longing are suppressed or repressed, they can show up in other ways, even if you are no longer in a relationship with that person. For example, you might long for a better life, deeper friendships, a career that can satisfy you, more money, or freedom. So whether this relationship is new or old it is important to take the time to CLEANSE what is showing up right now.

Clear Reactivity You can approach this exercise in one of two ways. You can do some cat-cow stretches by getting on your hands and knees in a tabletop position. Tilt your head and tailbone up at the same time as you inhale through your nose. On the exhale, tuck your chin and tailbone as you press your navel toward your spine. Or, if you prefer, you can do the same movement while sitting in a chair feet hip-width apart with your hands on your thighs. Either way you will tilt your spine, drop your belly, lift the crown of your head and tail, and round your spine as you pull your navel in, tucking your chin and tailbone. Repeat this sequence two or three times before you proceed to step two.

Look Inward How I feel in my body right now is . . . inhale through your nose . . . exhale through your nose.

Having this feeling of missing and longing activated inside me now makes me feel . . . inhale . . . exhale . . .

When I miss our sense of connection, it makes me feel . . . inhale . . . exhale . . .

Carrying this feeling in my heart now makes me feel . . . inhale . . . exhale . . .

Emit Hum three times.

Activate See it! Visualize an image of patience, balance, tranquility, purposefulness, and certainty. Perhaps the way it would feel to plant tomato seeds in a pot or garden.

Nourish Feel it! Imagine what patience and purposeful feels like. How you would have to relax and trust the plant's growth process and the purposefulness you'd feel harvesting your first tomato.

Surrender Say: "I allow patience. I allow hope. I allow harmony. I allow purpose. I allow calm. I allow trust."

Ease Say: "I am trusting. I am growth. I am purpose. I am patient. I am free."

Cleansing When You Feel Unappreciated

Appreciation is a funny thing. Some people feel appreciated when you tell them you are grateful for what they do; others feel it when you show them how you feel, maybe with flowers or a compliment; and some people feel appreciated by the way you treat them, like not taking their kindness or help for granted. When you feel unappreciated it is likely you are suppressing emotions of insecurity, unlikableness, or unworthiness. While feeling unappreciated can certainly contribute to emotional distress and conflict, it can also be an opportunity for connection. Once you CLEANSE what is showing up, I encourage you to let the people in your life know when you do feel appreciated. It may be as simple as saying thank you for a ride, a favor, or a phone call. While you might be inclined to want to wait until that person makes you feel better, this rarely works in your favor. Instead, choose to CLEANSE and see how your processed emotions can give you the energy to see the good around you.

Clear Reactivity Sit next to an open window or go outside and sit in a favorite spot. With your peace-sign fingers press each of these three points above your navel for two counts per press: about an inch above, one inch to the right of your navel, and one inch to the left. Let the breeze create some movement in the atmosphere.

Look Inward How I feel in my body right now is . . . inhale through your nose . . . exhale through your nose.

Not being appreciated makes me feel . . . inhale . . . exhale . . .

When the things I do and say go unnoticed, it makes me feel . . . inhale . . . exhale . . .

Cultivating a sense of appreciation within myself now makes me feel . . . inhale . . . exhale . . .

Emit Hum three times.

Activate See it! Visualize an image of value, respect, and esteem. Perhaps a beautiful thank-you card with some kind words.

Nourish Feel it! Imagine what it would feel like to unseal the envelope of this card and to read it to yourself. Imagine smiling while you read it.

Surrender Say: "I allow admiration. I allow respect. I allow cherishing. I allow presence. I allow esteem."

Ease Say: "I am appreciated. I am noticed. I am respected. I am cherished. I am free."

Cleansing Self-Consciousness

Have you ever gone shopping and tried on an outfit and thought you looked damn good until your partner or friend made a face as you walked out of the dressing room? Rather than be confident in the choice you made or the way the outfit made you feel, you headed back and changed. Maybe you were at a party with your significant other when someone far more attractive and confident than you walked into the room, leaving you with a feeling of no longer being special or good enough. While it might seem like this CLEANSE belongs in Part I: Self & Everyday Life, I find most of our insecurities are revealed through relationships. It is through our relationships with others that we become most aware of suppressed emotions of sadness, insecurity, and embarrassment.

If you do not CLEANSE these emotions you never get a chance to transform them into higher energy so that you can develop the courage and confidence available to you. That energy is always there, but you need to tap into it. While society tends to praise how we appear on the outside, as you practice this CLEANSE you will come to appreciate how having a sense of inner confidence makes you feel and even look more attractive. Trust me, people will notice. Now that I've got you on board and you are aware of what we are aiming for, let's CLEANSE.

Clear Reactivity Place the palm of your right hand over your navel. Sit up with your feet hip-width apart. Make the sound "ram ram ram" two or three times in a row. This is basic mantra and when combined, the sound of these syllables sends a vibration to your core. Pause, notice your breath, and proceed to step two.

Look Inward How I feel in my body right now is . . . inhale through your nose . . . exhale through your nose . . .

When I compare myself to others, it makes me feel . . . inhale . . . exhale . . .

A sense of insecurity around others makes me feel . . . inhale . . . exhale . . .

Not feeling good enough makes me feel . . . inhale . . . exhale . . .

Emit Hum three times.

Activate See it! Visualize an image of confidence. Perhaps a tall building with interesting architectural details or a musician or singer performing onstage for an enthusiastic audience.

Nourish Feel it! Imagine what it would feel like to fully trust your strength, energy, and abilities. Imagine you are the one onstage. How would you feel? Notice the way you are standing and moving, how you inhabit your body.

Surrender Say: "I allow freedom. I allow expression. I allow confidence. I allow energy. I allow me."

Ease Say: "I am me. I am energy. I am enough. I am confident. I am free."

Cleansing When You Have Little Time for Others

Do remember a time you felt like you were spread way too thin? Or maybe you are feeling that way right now. Your mind, energy, and attention are tugged in many different directions. Maybe you have a lot on your plate, you are trying to balance too much at once, are working long hours, or you have been preoccupied by your own personal issues to the point of anxiety. Inside you know this may be unfairly impacting your relationships with others, especially the people who depend on you. Perhaps there is a part of you that feels guilty or remorseful about that. Maybe you are starting to feel as if no matter how hard you work it will never be enough, so why bother? Instead of being hard on yourself, I strongly encourage you to CLEANSE. Notice what might be coming up emotionally for you through these thoughts—it will likely be something deeper than your to-do list. If you give yourself a chance to CLEANSE it will help flush out what is bothering you, allowing you to free yourself and become more connected to others.

Clear Reactivity Press both of your pinkie fingers together in front of your chest area. Your palms will be facing you and your other fingers will curl inward. Continue to press the pinkie fingers together as you breathe slowly through your nose, inflating your abdomen on the inhale and deflating it on exhale. Repeat this two or three times in a row. Release your fingers and proceed to step two.

Look Inward How I feel in my body right now is . . . inhale through your nose . . . exhale through your nose.

Having little time for others makes me feel . . . inhale . . . exhale . . .

When I think about taking time off, it makes me feel . . . inhale . . . exhale . . .

When I am too busy to spend time with the people I care about and love, it makes me feel . . . inhale . . . exhale . . .

Emit Hum three times.

Activate See it! Visualize an image of happiness, blessings, goodness, and simplicity. Maybe it's sitting quietly by a window overlooking a beautiful view or on a rock by a flowing stream. Where would you be?

Nourish Feel it! Imagine feeling what it would be like to be truly present to yourself right now. Sink into that feeling of sitting with goodness and simplicity.

Surrender Say: "I allow ease. I allow presence. I allow calm. I allow blessings. I allow good fortune. I allow connection."

Ease Say: "I am joy. I am ease. I am present. I am enough. I am blessing. I am happy. I am free."

Part III

FAMILY & HOME LIFE

Families are powerful indicators of patterns of reactivity—**nature combines with nurture to suppress emotions.** When emotions are processed, everyone is provided with a safe place to heal and grow.

L et's face it, when our family is in turmoil it can rock the boat like nothing else. I always feel like I can accomplish quite a lot of things in life . . . at least until one of my family members gets sick, is in trouble, or needs a helping hand. While family is often such a blessing, it can come with its fair share of challenges, so as you move through this category, remember this: each time you CLEANSE, you are not only relieving and healing yourself from toxic suppressed emotions and the damage they can do, but this healing will radiate, affecting your family members, and make for a happier home.

Here is the thing, the emotions belonging to the people in your family of origin or choice are often interwoven into the reactive patterns you enact. Therefore, when you choose to relinquish your part of the pattern (via feeling and detoxing) the change will impact not only you, but everyone close to you. Those of you who are used to putting everyone else first can quit that counterproductive misperception right now! Focusing on yourself and taking time to CLEANSE is a way to serve, love, and heal not just yourself but others.

Cleansing Family Get-Togethers

One of my CLEANSE students shared a story of how her mother tried to help her with Thanksgiving dinner preparations by putting the turkey in the oven early. When my student got home from working a late nightshift the turkey was burned. Even though she was fuming inside she did not want to spoil Thanksgiving for her kids or mom, so for the remainder of the day she put on a happy face and pretended she liked overcooked turkey.

There is no doubt life with family can be quite interesting. While these situations may give you a good chuckle later on, in the heat of the moment (particularly after a long day) they can cause conflict, tension, and hard feelings. Throw some politics and alcohol into the mix and gatherings with your family can reach a whole new level of reactivity. Before you know it a casual comment leads to an argument, and who knows what will happen next? Without CLEANSE, these festive celebrations can become nightmares, leaving us feeling more than a little rough around the edges. After all, it takes a lot of work, time, and preparation to pull these gatherings off and we do it because we want to, but we want it to be a positive experience for everyone. This CLEANSE is also a good one to revisit after a family vacation, heated phone call, or triggering conversation.

Clear Reactivity Standing up tall or lying flat on your back on the floor, draw one knee in toward your core. Think of it like giving your quadriceps a stretch. If you have some instability in your knees or ankles lying on the floor or in bed may be better for you. Otherwise, stand up, hold the wall if you need to, and draw one knee in at a time for twenty seconds on each side. Breathe.

Look Inward How I feel in my body right now is . . . inhale through your nose . . . exhale through your nose.

Being around family makes me feel . . . inhale . . . exhale . . .

When there is disagreement or tension, I feel . . . inhale . . . exhale . . .

When alcohol, politics, or parenting choices are added into the mix, it makes me feel . . . inhale . . . exhale . . .

Emit Hum three times.

Activate See it! Visualize an image of an activity that is relaxed, happy, calm, and content. Where would it be for you? Perhaps doing something you love, like fishing, biking, reading, or taking a nap.

Nourish Feel it! Imagine engaging in that activity right now. Tune in to how it would resonate in your body. The way your hands would feel on the handlebars of your bike, the rod of the fishing pole, or turning the pages of a book.

Surrender Say: "I allow peace. I allow differences. I allow

132

disagreements. I allow healing. I allow agreements. I allow boundaries. I allow flexibility."

~~~~~~

Ease Say: "I am flexible. I am healing. I am resilient. I am compassionate. I am understanding. I am calm. I am free."

Cleansing Travel

Traveling by train, airplane, or car for an extended period of time can take its toll physically—we're stiff from sitting in one position—and mentally—we just want to be there already and not worry about missed connections or the weather. Throw a couple of tired, cranky, or restless kids into the mix and the tension can escalate. God forbid you or another adult in the car loses it even for a moment and threatens to pull the car over or cancel the trip altogether, then you are really in for a fun ride . . . or not. Here is the thing, you need oxygen and circulation to transform some of those congested emotions that are showing up for you. So if you are planning a trip, I highly recommend you take a picture of this page or copy down this CLEANSE and bring it with you. Move through the steps both before, after, and even during your trip in rest areas or before you go to sleep.

Clear Reactivity Before you hit the road be sure to slowly drink a glass of cool water preferably with ice. Swallowing this water and causing a temperature shift will tone your vagus nerve. Be sure to take a moment to shake out your legs, maybe stretch a bit before getting back into the car or boarding the plane.

Look Inward How I feel in my body right now is . . . inhale through your nose . . . exhale through your nose.

Sitting for extended periods of time makes me feel . . . inhale . . . exhale . . .

Being away from home makes me feel . . . inhale . . . exhale . . .

When my family is discontent, it makes me feel . . . inhale . . . exhale . . .

When things get complicated or don't go according to plan it makes me feel . . . inhale . . . exhale . . .

Emit Hum three times.

Activate See it! Visualize an image of calm, poise, contentment, pleasure, and optimism. Perhaps an image of yourself whistling or casually strolling on a beautiful path through the woods or a garden.

Nourish Feel it! Imagine what it like to be whistling or strolling right now. How would your arms move? Notice if they feel loose and relaxed.

Surrender Say: "I allow nourishment. I allow grounding. I allow refreshing. I allow renewal. I allow presence."

Ease Say: "I am present. I am nourished. I am calm. I am grounded. I am relaxed. I am free."

Cleansing
Paying Bills

No doubt about it! Paying bills, especially the ones that are unexpected such as a medical bill or emergency home repair, can cause a lot of stress and anxiety. As a result, you may find yourself avoiding or putting off responding to certain statements or charges. Reactions such as worry, complaining, anger, or arguments can surface among family members around bill time. It can be so tempting to push blame or police each other's spending rather than tend to what you feel emotionally. This is one area in which things can escalate pretty quickly, sometimes to the point where you might even have to make some really hard choices like borrowing money or changing your lifestyle. The bottom line is, bills have a way of bringing up all sorts of unprocessed feelings. The reactivity is even worse now in households affected by the pandemic and rampant unemployment. Emotions such as unfairness, frustration, a sense of lack or of being trapped may rise to the surface. If you get angry or lash out you will likely push those emotions right back down.

I know for me things like worry, questioning, complaining, and blame can easily surface. *Who in the heck purchased this? Why didn't you get the cheaper one?* Keep in mind reactions without awareness can suppress what is really trying to surface—emotions such as fear, frustration, resentment, the stress of providing for a family, or a sense of being overwhelmed. Without a CLEANSE things can escalate to the point where you might need to think about changing jobs, cutting off a necessary service, or switching doctors to avoid high payments. While some of those choices might be for the good, I do not recommend doing anything in the heat of the moment. If you act rashly and make an external shift without cleansing the internal issues you will likely push your feelings right back down. Remember emotions don't just disappear on their own, they need you to process them, which is what this CLEANSE is about.

Clear Reactivity Tone your vagus nerve by pressing your tongue on the roof of your closed mouth as you inhale . . . and exhale . . . through your nose. Keep your tongue pressed to the roof of your mouth as you take two or three more slow deep breaths.

Look Inward How I feel in my body right now is . . . inhale through your nose . . . exhale through your nose.

Paying this bill makes me feel . . . inhale . . . exhale . . .

Not paying this bill makes me feel . . . inhale . . . exhale . . .

Having this bill show up in my life now makes me feel . . . inhale . . . exhale . . .

Emit Hum three times.

Activate See it! Visualize being balanced, calm, undisturbed. Perhaps balancing rocks or still water in a birdbath.

Nourish Feel it! Notice how observing the birds playing in the water makes you feel inside your body. Can you connect to the energy of the birds calmly playing in the water?

Surrender Say: "I allow pure. I allow renewal. I allow abundance. I allow goodness. I allow honesty."

Ease Say: "I am honest. I am growing. I am clear. I am worthy. I am capable. I am goodness."

Cleansing When a Family Member Is Upset

I t is difficult to hide from our family or keep our feelings secret. This is because they are the people who know us best. If something is off or you seem out of sorts, a family member is likely to notice. In this CLEANSE, we will focus on your being around a family member who is upset. Maybe it is a small child who is sick, a teenager suffering their first heartbreak, or an adult child who didn't get into their dream college. Perhaps it is someone else you live with, such as your mother, partner, or even a roommate who has come to be like family.

Here is the challenging part: When it comes to family, part of you may want to help them feel better while another part of you wants to walk away—not because you are mean or a bad person but because their issue is creating discord among everyone in your home. Let's face it, home is that space where we hope to be able to relax, de-stress, and connect with one another, yet in reality this is often unrealistic. Human beings have emotions and reactions and it would be a bit of a reach to expect everyone to be calm, happy, and content all the time. With that said, a CLEANSE can help. Unless it is an emergency, consider this CLEANSE before you approach a family member to try to help. If you can't CLEANSE right away do it as soon as you remember.

Clear Reactivity On each hand, bring your fingers together to touch the thumb. Your hands will look a little like a bird's beak. This is a mudra that can promote balance and presence in all areas of your body. Hold the hand position for one minute while breathing in . . . and out . . . through your nose. Inflate your abdomen on the inhale and deflate on the exhale.

Look Inward How I feel in my body right now is . . . inhale through your nose . . . exhale through your nose.

When someone close to me is upset or stressed, it makes me feel . . . inhale . . . exhale . . .

When I do not know what to do or say, it makes me feel . . . inhale . . . exhale . . .

Emit Hum three times.

Activate See it! Visualize an image of something calm, soothing, smooth, and relaxed. Perhaps a smooth stone or silky piece of fabric.

Nourish Feel it! Imagine holding this stone in the palm of your hand and rubbing your thumb across the surface.

Surrender Say: "I allow calm. I allow soothing. I allow relaxing. I allow peace. I allow resolution."

Ease Say: "I am calm. I am fluid. I am grounded. I am soothed. I am at peace. I am love."

140

Cleansing Hyper-Focusing on Others

My neighbor pulled into the driveway, got out of his car, and the first thing that popped out of his mouth was to ask his wife about their son: "Did he go looking for a job today?" My neighbor's wife replied, "I don't know. Why don't you ask him?" The tension between them was evident and it was clear my neighbor had been ruminating during his drive home on whether their son had looked for a job.

Now ask yourself, have you been over focusing on a particular family member? Do you find yourself wanting to tell them what to do, give advice, make sure their homework is perfectly completed, or warn them about the problems they might encounter as they go about their day? Or maybe you are worried about a loved one's health and monitor how they are taking care of themselves, keeping up with their medication or doctors' visits. Here is the thing about overfocusing, without awareness it can put an enormous amount of energy and attention on what is not working or what you are afraid of as opposed to helping with solutions. Many people believe that what we focus on expands. In other words, you could be making the situation worse by focusing on what you are worrying about. CLEANSE the reaction of hyper-focusing to help with this.

Clear Reactivity Open your mouth wide for three seconds as if you were at the dentist, now release it. You may even hear your ears pop. Repeat two or three times and then swallow your saliva.

Look Inward How I feel in my body right now is . . . inhale through your nose . . . exhale through your nose.

When I notice what is wrong or what I do not like, it makes me feel . . . inhale . . . exhale . . . (Be sure to breathe slowly here. Inhale and count one . . . two . . . three . . . exhale and count one . . . two . . . three . . . so you can really dig up all the reactivity.)

Overfocusing on things in this way makes me feel . . . inhale . . . exhale . . .

When I become fixated on this situation or person, it makes me feel . . . inhale . . . exhale . . .

Emit Hum three times.

Activate See it! Visualize an image of hope, optimism, trust, and constructiveness. Perhaps you'll picture the rising sun or a full moon.

Nourish Feel it! Imagine what it would feel like to watch the sunrise or view the moonset. How might this stimulate sensations of hope and trust within you?

Surrender Say: "I allow hope. I allow purpose. I allow positivity. I allow sound. I allow calm."

Ease Say: "I am hope. I am purpose. I am positive. I am calm. I am sound. I am free."

Cleansing Time

Time is funny; we it need to create healthy routines and help us remember what in the heck day it is. *I have no time . . . There just aren't enough hours in the day . . . I wish I had a minute to spare.* How often have you heard yourself saying these things? I know I have. Without awareness (and a good CLEANSE) these statements could be an indication you are repressing emotions. Sure, on the outside it sounds like something anyone would say when they are juggling the activities and schedules of work or family life. Yet when you peel back the layers and start to CLEANSE, you realize statements such as these may really be code for *I feel overwhelmed . . . I feel pressured . . . I could really use a hand right now . . . I really need more time for myself.*

In this CLEANSE pay attention to the second step and let the discomfort from the initial sentence bubble up to the surface. Try not to rush to the hum.

Clear Reactivity Tilt your right ear toward your right shoulder, casting your gaze over your shoulder as you do this. Hold this stretch for one . . . two . . . three seconds. Repeat on the left side, left ear toward left shoulder as you cast your gaze to the left and downward, holding for a count of one . . . two . . . three.

Look Inward How I feel in my body right now is . . . inhale through your nose . . . exhale through your nose.

When it seems like there aren't enough hours in the day to accomplish all I need to do, it makes me feel . . . inhale . . . exhale . . .

Trying to fit everything in makes me feel . . . inhale . . . exhale . . .

Emit Hum three times.

Activate See it! Visualize an image of something relaxed, easygoing, calm, and cool. Perhaps floating in a boat in the middle of a lake or swinging in a hammock under some shady trees.

Nourish Feel it! Imagine sinking into the hammock and feeling it cocoon you in its an embrace. Feel the air.

Surrender Say: "I allow relaxed. I allow easygoing. I allow calm. I allow cool."

Ease Say: "I am relaxed. I am easygoing. I am calm. I am cool."

Cleansing Homework

Whether you are an adult taking classes to further your career or a teenager buried in assignments, having too much homework can contribute to anxiety and stress, particularly if you are having trouble understanding the information in the first place. When the workload seems unfair, irrelevant, or just plain boring, this can contribute to feelings of frustration and dread.

Over the years, I have heard many parents report how difficult it is to watch their children struggle, cry, and lose sleep over the thought of not being able to complete all their assignments. The challenge is that when there is too much homework due (even as an adult) other things fall by the wayside—like play, exercise, sleep, creative projects, and time with friends. While this is a big topic to cover, with lots of valid viewpoints, the purpose here is to CLEANSE all the reactivity that comes up around homework (both past and present) so you (and your child) can fully process those emotions.

Clear Reactivity Stand up and do about five jumping jacks. Yes, you read that correctly! Do five jumping jacks. If this is too much for you, modify the exercise by crossing your arms in front of your body back and forth several times in a row, alternating between crossing your arms and opening them up. The intention is to get your blood moving.

Look Inward How I feel in my body right now is . . . inhale through your nose . . . exhale through your nose.

Looking at homework makes me feel . . . inhale . . . exhale . . .

When I do not understand the homework, it makes me feel . . . inhale . . . exhale . . .

When I believe I won't be able to finish my homework, it makes me feel . . . inhale . . . exhale . . .

Emit Hum three times.

Activate See it! Visualize an image of calm, confidence, reassurance, focus, and clarity. Perhaps an image of looking through a clear window at a scenic view.

Nourish Feel it! Imagine what it would feel like to look out that window on a cloudless day. How does it feel in your body to be able to think and see clearly?

Surrender Say: "I allow relaxation. I allow being carefree. I allow chilling. I allow easygoing. I allow ease."

Ease Say: "I am capable. I am focused. I am breath. I am calm. I am confident. I am free."

Cleansing Grief

Grief is the process of moving through loss. It includes emotions such as shock, disbelief, anguish, pain, deep sorrow, anger, and despair. With that said, as with all emotions, many people deal with their grief in diverse ways. When grieving you may be quite good at understanding the importance of honoring what you feel. For example, you may allow yourself to take a few days off from work, limit your social media exposure, or give yourself permission to cry. Conversely, you may find yourself in reactivity, shocked by the news and determined to stay strong so that your emotions do not "get in the way" as you allow the sorrow to percolate.

While there is no right or wrong way to grieve, a CLEANSE can support the process. For example, anger during grief can be healthy, yet if it goes on too long, interferes with your health, relationships, or your ability to process how you feel about a loss, you ought to consider including this CLEANSE in your daily routine for as long as you feel you need it.

Clear Reactivity Place a small damp towel or washcloth in the dryer or in the microwave. Allow it to heat up (be careful it is not too hot so you don't burn yourself) and then take it out and wrap it around the back of your neck and shoulders. If you don't have access to a dryer or microwave, wrap yourself up in a soft blanket or cozy afghan. Leave it there as you move through this CLEANSE.

Look Inward How I feel in my body right now is . . . inhale through your nose . . . exhale through your nose.

Tuning in to my heart now makes me feel . . . inhale . . . exhale . . .

Breathing in makes me feel . . . inhale . . . exhale . . .

Breathing out makes me feel . . . inhale . . . exhale . . .

Emit Place your hand on your heart and hum three times.

Activate See it! Visualize warmth, light, ease, and comfort such as a flickering candlelight or the sunlight peeking through the clouds

Nourish Feel it! Imagine what it would feel like to feel the sun shine on the nape of your neck, the way it would caress your shoulders and warm you.

Surrender Say: "I allow light. I allow glow. I allow connection. I allow healing. I allow ease."

Ease Say: "I am healing. I am connected. I am source. I am light. I am hope. I am free."

Cleansing
Holidays

The holidays can bring about a host of mixed emotions. There might be a part of you that looks forward to them and enjoys the opportunity to spread some cheer, while another part of you might wish you could skip them altogether because holidays can bring on extra pressure with all the tasks, responsibilities, obligations, changes in your routine, and expectations. As a result, you may be at the point where you are ready to loosen the reins a bit, cut back on all the spending, but another part of you is looking to kick it up a notch and make the holidays extra special.

No matter how you choose to celebrate, this CLEANSE can help you through the holidays by easing some of the stress and helping you to handle whatever triggers might come your way. You know the ones I mean—the ones that make you feel annoyed or heated. Like Aunt Alice's comment about your cooking or the things that come out of Uncle Al's mouth when he has had too many drinks. While you can't always control what happens during the holidays, you can CLEANSE the experience. As you do, don't be surprised if your experiences around the season changes for the better. This is a good CLEANSE to do before and after your holiday activities. And if things get really rough, excuse yourself from the table and do this CLEANSE in the middle of the festivities!

Clear Reactivity Interlace your fingers behind your head as you sit or stand up tall. Tilt your head into your hands and let them support the weight as if you were kicking back in a hammock. Inhale through your nose and then release your jaw while making an "aah" sound aloud. Repeat two or three times. Bring your head back to center, release your hands and arms, and notice your breath.

Look Inward How I feel in my body right now is . . . inhale through your nose . . . exhale through your nose.

Attending holiday gatherings makes me feel . . . inhale . . . exhale . . .

Beginning the holiday process makes me feel . . . inhale . . . exhale . . .

When the holidays come to an end, it makes me feel . . . inhale . . . exhale . . .

Emit Hum three times.

Activate See it! Visualize an image of balance, calm, cheer, and rejuvenation. Imagine an image of snow melting away to reveal an early spring flower.

Nourish Feel it! Imagine the sensation (e.g. flutter) inside your body when you notice the early signs of spring.

Surrender Say: "I allow rejuvenation. I allow balance. I am new growth. I allow melting. I allow refresh."

Ease Say: "I am rejuvenating. I am balanced. I am purified. I am serenity. I am at peace."

Cleansing Chores

Chores—doing laundry, going grocery shopping, cleaning the toilet, taking out the trash, emptying the dishwasher, or running errands—can be pleasant or unpleasant, yet they are necessary tasks. While some people might enjoy raking the leaves or vacuuming, others may find them to be a complete pain or nuisance.

If you are wondering how a CLEANSE can help both you and your family tackle the household chores, let me tell you a story. I once asked one of my teenage daughters what was getting in the way of keeping her room clean. Do you know what she said? "Honestly, Mom, if I leave it long enough I don't see the mess anymore. I get used to it." *Huh?* Interesting. In that moment, I knew that rather than remind, lecture, or bribe my daughter, I had something to CLEANSE. It looked something like, "When she doesn't see the mess it makes me feel . . . inhale . . . exhale . . ." You get the point.

Clear Reactivity Here, I encourage you to sink into your exhale. Sit or stand up tall, close your eyes, and let gravity take over, pulling your navel toward your spine. Take a nice long exhale and to make it a little extra deep, squeeze the muscles of your pelvic floor. For

153

women this will be a slight Kegel. Hold that squeeze for two or three seconds and then release as you allow your breath to flow. Repeat this sequence—squeeze . . . breathe—two or three more times. (Note: If you are pregnant, don't hold your breath at all.)

Look Inward How I feel in my body right now is . . . inhale through your nose . . . exhale through your nose.

Cleaning up messes makes me feel . . . inhale . . . exhale . . .

Not cleaning up messes makes me feel . . . inhale . . . exhale . . .

When things get disorganized or out of control, it makes me feel . . . inhale . . . exhale . . .

When other people do not do their part, it makes me feel . . . inhale . . . exhale . . .

Emit Hum three times.

Activate See it! Visualize an image of satisfaction. Perhaps enjoying a nourishing meal or finally exploring a neighborhood, park, or trail you'd always been curious about.

Nourish Feel it! Notice how it feels in your lower abdomen when you have eaten something delicious and savor the satisfaction, contentment, and pleasure.

Surrender Say: "I allow awareness. I allow energy. I allow motivation. I allow support. I allow completion. I allow freedom."

Ease Say: "I am aware. I am complete. I am calm. I am upbeat. I am efficient. I am motivated. I am free."

Cleansing
Put-Downs

You may have been raised by someone who put you down or even bullied you. Maybe you had a sibling who teased you a lot or talked poorly about you to their friends. Or perhaps you married someone who was put down by their mother or father when they were growing up. Even if you were not the recipient of the put-downs, I often find we are drawn to partners, friends, and even teachers who have suppressed emotions that are similar to ours.

A CLEANSE can help you shift the unconscious emotional energy patterns that live inside you. If you were the one who was put down, moving through this CLEANSE will help you purify some of those irrational beliefs you might have developed about yourself along the way. Things like, "He is my brother, so he is supposed to love me unconditionally and be kind." Or, "I must have been a pretty bad child for my mother to treat me that way." You can find that unconditional space of love, forgiveness, and acceptance you may be longing for if you process your emotions. Since so many of us have learned to withhold, project, or act out when we're struggling emotionally, receiving the benefits of this CLEANSE will be a new experience.

Clear Reactivity Take off your shoes so you can rub the bottoms of your feet. Yes, you read that right: Go ahead and rub the inner arches of both of your feet. Spend about one minute per foot. Be sure to dig in with your thumbs as you knead the muscle back and forth. Then, sit up tall and observe your breathing.

Look Inward How I feel in my body right now is . . . inhale through your nose . . . exhale through your nose.

When I was called names or made fun of, it made me feel . . . inhale . . . exhale . . .

Carrying these beliefs in myself now makes me feel . . . inhale . . . exhale . . .

Emit Hum three times.

Activate See it! Visualize an image of fluidity such as water pouring from a pitcher into a glass. Observe the way the liquid moves effortlessly from one container into another. The container receiving the water is symbolic of the new you—pure, fresh, clean, and refilled.

Nourish Feel it! Imagine what it would feel like in your body to hold that pitcher of water, sensing its weight lighten as you transfer the contents into a new container. Imagine pouring with a steady hand, and with that same level of ease imagine taking charge of your emotional energy.

Surrender Say: "I allow release. I allow purity. I allow cleansing. I allow relief. I allow whole."

Ease Say: "I am released. I am pure. I am cleansed. I am whole. I am light. I am free."

Cleansing
Projection

As she packed up her beach chairs, sand toys, towels, and tote bag, my friend heard herself ranting to her children: "If you (notice the "you" word) guys want to do this again then you better start helping out." In the middle of all the ruckus she dropped her keys, and clearly at the end of her rope lashed out, "Kids, when we get home you are getting a consequence!" Projection is a reaction. It generally happens when your unresolved, unprocessed emotions externalize themselves in rather abrupt ways. As a result you may find yourself projecting (directing) what you feel toward something or someone else. This makes you want to do things like slam the door or end an activity (like leaving the beach) right away.

Some people get hooked into the reaction of projection because it can actually give you a temporary relief (through venting, yelling, etc.) of pent-up emotions. The challenge is that this does not lead to resolution or positive change. Emotions do not get processed from projecting; they get processed when we CLEANSE.

Clear Reactivity Keeping your palms apart, press all ten fingertips together until you sense an energetic connection or warmth. Hold your hands in this position as you inhale slowly through your nose and inflate your abdomen . . . and exhale as you release your abdomen. Repeat this sequence two or three times.

Look Inward How I feel in my body right now is . . . inhale through your nose . . . exhale through your nose.

When I feel a strong energy inside me, it makes me feel . . . inhale . . . exhale . . .

Holding this energy in makes me feel . . . inhale . . . exhale . . .

Letting this energy release now makes me feel . . . inhale . . . exhale . . .

Emit Hum three times.

Activate See it! Visualize a level and vast horizon. Perhaps a desert, a wide-open beach, or a long boardwalk.

Nourish Feel it! Imagine walking through the landscape, feeling the evenness of the earth underneath you. As you take each step notice how the energy in your body feels balanced and even.

Surrender Say: "I allow digested emotions. I allow even. I allow balance. I allow calm. I allow gentle flow. I allow rhythm."

Ease Say: "I am digesting emotions. I am even. I am balanced. I am calm. I am gentle. I am in flow. I am free."

Cleansing Poor Choices

I remember picking up my daughter one day from an after-school activity. She got in the car and said, "Mom you are not going to believe it, Annie and Scott purposely clogged the toilet with toilet paper." This is an example of a poor choice. Young and old we have all been there. It might be about financial decisions, travel plans, purchases, or simply blurting out an opinion without thinking it through. Whether you are the one who initiated the poor choice or were a bystander, this CLEANSE will help relieve whatever emotions were suppressed that day.

You see, when you make a poor choice you might not realize the consequences of your actions as you engage in them. In the heat of the moment it is easy to get caught up in the excitement, outrage, or even hope, without the necessary emotional processing. If you act in ways you later regret, these situations can find ways to bury themselves inside of you, hindering your ability to move forward, connect, or forgive yourself for what you did or did not do at the time.

Clear Reactivity Roll your shoulders up toward your ears then bring them back and forward. Really exaggerate this movement, making as big of a circle as you can. Repeat this stretch three times in a row. Pause, breathe, and then do another three or four shoulder circles. Pause, breathe, and move to step two.

Look Inward How I feel in my body right now is . . . inhale through your nose . . . exhale through your nose.

When I look back at that moment, it makes me feel . . . inhale . . . exhale . . .

Connecting to what I was feeling during that time now makes me feel . . . inhale . . . exhale . . .

Emit Hum three times.

Activate See it! Visualize an image of relief, comfort, ease, gentleness, and compassion. Perhaps an image of soft rain or fog in a colorful garden.

Nourish Feel it! Imagine what it would feel like to stand in the rain, to experience the sensation of the moisture touching your arms and face.

Surrender Say: "I allow new beginnings. I allow comfort. I allow movement. I allow ease."

Ease Say: "I am new beginnings. I am comfort. I am real. I am raw. I am growing. I am ease."

Cleansing When You Feel Like You Put in an Unfair Amount of Effort

A relationship is a state of connection and with family that's doubled. That connection influences the energy underlying how you behave, how you feel, and how think around one another. Yet, if one person in the family feels they are putting more effort in than another, it can create strain and disharmony even among the most loving individuals. People often talk about how relationships require work, and while in many cases that may be true, I believe more so that relationships require feeling and empathy.

You see, without taking time to process your emotions, old reactive patterns can seep into your relationships and poison them. It is

161

not how much work you are doing or not doing, but rather how are you coping with the feelings that are coming up? Do you manage by trying harder or taking on more? Are you playing the martyr? Or do you manage your anxiety by doing as little as possible? And how do you know when you cross the line from self-care to avoidance? The dynamics between you and your family members can give you quite a bit of information about the ways you may be avoiding processing your own emotions.

Clear Reactivity Lie down on your back on the floor. Draw your right knee into your chest as you keep the other leg nice and long. Inhale . . . and exhale. Now move into a gentle spinal twist by drawing your right knee over to the left, keeping your shoulders on the floor. You can bring your right arm out to the side to help ground you. Return to center and straighten your spine as you press it gently to the floor. Switch legs and draw your left knee toward your chest, right leg extended. Breathe and draw your left knee over to the right as you gently twist your spine. Use your left arm to ground you. Return to center and while settled on the floor or after you sit up, move on to the next step.

Look Inward How I feel in my body right now is . . . inhale through your nose . . . exhale through your nose.

When I feel like my needs are not being met, it makes me feel . . . inhale . . . exhale . . .

Wanting things to change for the better makes me feel . . . inhale . . . exhale . . .

Emit Hum three times.

Activate See it! Visualize an image of encouragement, fulfillment, love, and compassion. Where would you go in nature to feel supported and fortified? Perhaps a rose garden filled with pink, red, and yellow roses.

162

Nourish Feel it! How would it feel to be hopeful and encouraged? Perhaps you might breathe a little easier, feel a bit calmer and lighter.

Surrender Say: "I allow hope. I allow compassion. I allow understanding. I allow encouragement. I allow support. I allow appreciation. I allow fulfillment."

Ease Say: "I am love. I am appreciation. I am fulfillment. I am empathy. I am compassion. I am grace."

Cleansing
Homesickness

Have you ever had a time when you longed for the comforts of home? The familiarity of your own bed, the smell of food in the kitchen, or the solace and easy communication of being around family members? Maybe you were on a business trip or a solo vacation. While there is no perfect family, there may be times when you actually miss the imperfections of being at home. Absence does indeed make the heart grow fonder, and when you miss your family and home, even the things that annoy you can bring a smile to your face. Things like how stubborn your sister can be about sharing her clothes or the way your mother has to insist on a family photo every time you gather. Right now, home may be a place where you reside, a spot in nature that holds an important place in your heart, or a community you return to now and then because it holds such wonderful memories. Home can carry the memories of hardship or challenges, but it can also bring back simple recollections of long, healing walks and conversations, hugs for no reason, or what it is like to sit down and enjoy a glass of lemonade in companionable silence. While reflecting on home can bring up all sorts of things for you, in this CLEANSE you will focus on releasing any reactivity around the emotions of what it's like to feel homesick.

Clear Reactivity Curl all eight fingers toward your palms. Holding this position, place your hands on your lap or a table in front of you. Point your thumbs toward each other, but do not let them touch. Keep a space of about an inch between your hands. Take two or three slow deep breaths as you inhale through your nose and inflate your abdomen . . . exhale through your nose as you deflate your abdomen and pause in this position for a moment. Release. Pause, and move to step two.

Look Inward How I feel in my body right now is . . . inhale through your nose . . . exhale through your nose.

When I think of home, it makes me feel . . . inhale . . . exhale . . .

When I reflect on family, it makes me feel . . . inhale . . . exhale . . .

Emit Hum three times.

Activate See it! Visualize in your mind's eye the image of presence, continuation, completion, and love. Perhaps a nest with chirping baby birds snuggled inside.

Nourish Feel it! Imagine observing that nest right now. What do you sense? Can you smell the air?

Surrender Say: "I allow presence. I allow comfort. I allow energy. I allow change. I allow connection. I allow love."

Ease Say: "I am present. I am change. I am love. I am existence. I am complete."

Cleansing Annoyance

When left unprocessed, annoyance is a reaction that can really get under your skin. Think of it as similar to having an itch in the middle of your back—it can be difficult to reach on your own, especially without a CLEANSE to process the emotions causing it. When it comes to family, it is not uncommon to be irritated by the same conversations (*Seriously? That story again*), behaviors, habits, and mindsets. You might wish things were different, perhaps "If only my sister had married a better guy, family vacations could be fun instead of an ordeal" or "If only my mother would listen to advice, her life would be a lot easier and less stressful and so would mine!" Whether you are mildly aggravated or at the end of your rope, consider this CLEANSE. Unprocessed annoyance can build and fester and becomes something far worse—an outburst, an argument, or an estrangement.

Clear Reactivity Sit up nice and tall with your feet hip-width apart. Take off your shoes and socks. Move both feet in a circular motion—clockwise for the count of six . . . counterclockwise for the count of six—as you loosen your ankle joint and tight muscles. Now, spread your toes, and then scrunch them up as you allow your breath to kick in and inhale for one . . . two . . . three . . . and exhale for one . . . two . . . three.

Look Inward How I feel in my body right now is . . . inhale through your nose . . . exhale through your nose.

Rolling my ankles in this way makes me feel . . . inhale . . . exhale . . .

Breathing through these triggers now makes me feel . . . inhale . . . exhale . . .

Having to deal with this situation makes me feel . . . inhale . . . exhale . . .

Emit Hum three times.

Activate See it! Visualize an image of something lovely, reassuring, and calm. Perhaps completing a satisfying task like weeding a flower bed.

Nourish Feel it! Imagine allowing yourself to really enjoy that experience. Take your time and focus on the things you love.

Surrender Say: "I allow warmth. I allow space. I allow calm. I allow freedom. I allow peace."

Ease Say: "I am calm. I am spacious. I am soothed. I am at peace."

Cleansing
Political
Differences

When it comes to both our immediate and extended families, there are some topics we all tend to avoid, and politics is usually one of them. While some people might enjoy a good debate about our government, how it should be run, and who should be in charge, others might find divergent opinions to be combative, offensive, or even alienating. If you have been around family members who have strong differences of opinion that led to discord and friction in the family you will benefit from this CLEANSE. You might also consider this CLEANSE if you plan on visiting family members whose politics are likely to be a conversation topic (particularly after a few cocktails), and you may already have concerns or judgments—reactions—before you even get together. I rarely meet someone who isn't stirred up by politics; it is such a heated topic in our world, so quite frankly, we could all use a little CLEANSE in this area.

Clear Reactivity Sit up tall in a chair or crossed-legged on the floor. Look forward and keep your chin parallel to the ground as you drop your shoulders back and down. Gently twist to the right, placing your left hand outside your right knee. Breathe in . . . and out . . . through your nose one or two times. Change sides by twisting to the left and placing your right hand outside your left knee. Breathe.

Look Inward How I feel in my body right now is . . . inhale through your nose . . . exhale through your nose.

Being around opposing political views makes me feel . . . inhale . . . exhale . . .

When I try to assert my views, it makes me feel . . . inhale . . . exhale . . .

Holding back my true feelings makes me feel . . . inhale . . . exhale . . .

Emit Hum three times.

Activate See it! Visualize an image of that is open, spacious, harmonious, and settling. Perhaps you see yourself sitting on a large rock overlooking a beautiful valley.

Nourish Feel it! Take in the vastness of this view, feel it in your bones, on your skin, and appreciate how open and expansive it feels.

Surrender Say: "I allow open. I allow harmony. I allow observation. I allow watching. I allow acceptance. I allow vastness."

Ease Say: "I am open. I am expansive. I am transformative. I am observant. I am accepting. I am free."

Cleansing Mis-communication

Have you ever asked someone about a plan and received few (if any) details in return? Or maybe you got the plan after persisting, but somehow it was changed. Or you received the information secondhand. Perhaps you were trying to figure out what was going on from one long, convoluted scroll of texts. Here is the thing about miscommunication: The person who is the last one to know kind of gets the short end of the stick. There is nothing worse than being on a different page than everyone else. It is like being given different directions to the same location, except the ones you received included a few detours. While occasional miscommunications happen—an unclear text or a comment taken the wrong way—when they become regular occurrences this can lead to distrust, bitterness, and hurt. To be sure these divergences do not completely waste your time or energy or trigger bigger emotions, take an opportunity to CLEANSE.

Clear Reactivity Stand up tall with your feet about hip-width apart, chin parallel to the ground. Take your two peace-sign fingers and press gently about an inch above your navel as you hold the pressure for a count of one . . . two . . . and then move about an inch to the right and press for a count of one . . . two . . . and then an inch to the left, again pressing press for a count of one . . . two. After you have pressed three times, stretch your neck to the right and to the left, and remember to breathe before you move to step two.

Look Inward How I feel in my body right now is . . . inhale through your nose . . . exhale through your nose.

When I feel confused about the plan, it makes me feel . . . inhale . . . exhale . . .

Communicating with my family in this way makes me feel . . . inhale . . . exhale . . .

When the information gets distorted or confusing, it makes me feel . . . inhale . . . exhale . . .

When I am left out of the conversation, it makes me feel . . . inhale . . . exhale . . .

Emit Hum three times.

Activate See it! Visualize an image of clarity, understanding, insight, and validation. Maybe it's someone making eye contact and nodding in agreement as they listen to you speak.

Nourish Feel it! What would direct communication feel like in your body?

Surrender Say: "I allow validation. I allow focus. I allow clarity. I allow listening. I allow speaking."

Ease Say: "I am speaking. I am listening. I am communicating. I am eye contact. I am clarity."

Cleansing Overscheduling

These days it is not uncommon for families to become overwhelmingly busy with activities on the weekends as well as throughout the week. Things like our children's test prep tutors, sports practices, and music lessons—not to mention the work we brought home on Friday—can leave little time for relaxing things like getting together with neighbors, playdates, home cooking, and leisurely activities such as going for a walk or playing a board game. While some families prefer having a packed schedule, it can take its toll physically and emotionally and can be used to suppress emotions. This is because emotions process better when you are not on the run and have time to look at them and CLEANSE. Since emotions require awareness, they need you to pause long enough and be present. If you are unsure what to cut out or you have been in this overscheduled rhythm for a long time, consider adding this CLEANSE to your routine. You can even move through the steps in your car while you wait for your children to

Clear Reactivity Get into a comfortable seated position and place your hands together in prayer pose, directly in front of your heart center. As you press your palms together, allow your gaze to fall to the ground while your chin remains parallel to the floor. Inhale through your nose . . . one . . . two . . . and exhale through your nose as you bring your navel toward your spine. Notice how placing your hands in front of your heart focuses you. Sit with this for about thirty seconds and then move to step two.

Look Inward How I feel in my body right now is . . . inhale through your nose . . . exhale through your nose.

Holding the space in front of my heart center now makes me feel . . . inhale . . . exhale . . .

When my mind and body are running in different directions, it makes me feel . . . inhale . . . exhale . . .

Taking this moment now makes me feel . . . inhale . . . exhale . . .

Emit Hum three times.

Activate See it! Visualize an image of something carefree, relaxed, and easy. Perhaps an image of footprints in the sand or the feeling of a few smooth pebbles in your hand.

Nourish Feel it! Look around you right now. Notice anything in the moment that connects you to nature—the sky through the window, a tree, or a potted plant. Notice how you feel in your body when you pause to pay attention.

Surrender Say: "I allow breath. I allow centering. I allow tuning in. I allow openness. I allow freedom."

Ease Say: "I am open. I am free. I am relaxed. I am soothed. I am breath."

Cleansing When You Lose Your Pet

Pets are like family. I, for one, frequently refer to my cat as my son. With three daughters in our house he is the closest to having a boy child I am going to get. When our pets are hurt, sick, missing, or aging it can be incredibly heartbreaking. I once met a man who had to move out of his home because the memories of his dog were too painful. You can do this CLEANSE if a pet is sick, you know the end is near, or they have passed away. It can help you through a difficult time and release the emotions attached to those creatures that give us so much unconditional love.

Clear Reactivity Tone your vagus nerve by either giving someone else a one-minute hug or wrapping your arms around yourself and giving yourself a one-minute hug. Be sure to use all sixty seconds and make it a good squeeze. Pause, place your hands in your lap, and move to step two.

Look Inward How I feel in my body right now is . . . inhale through your nose . . . exhale through your nose.

When I think about my pet, it makes me feel inhale . . . exhale . . .

Tuning into these thoughts and feelings now makes me feel . . . inhale . . . exhale . . .

Emit Hum three times.

Activate See it! Visualize an image of release, surrender, love, and completion. Perhaps an image of a beautiful star twinkling through the branches at the top of a tree. Sit back and let that star shine.

Nourish Feel it! Imagine what it would feel like to surrender as you release whatever it is you may be holding in your body. Offer yourself a nice, long, purifying sigh.

Surrender Say: "I allow release. I allow healing. I allow love. I allow surrender. I allow completion."

Ease Say: "I am love. I am surrender. I am healing. I am present. I am free."

Cleansing Power Struggles

If you are a parent and ask your child to do something and they refuse, you know what it is like to be in a power struggle. Perhaps you are an adult feeling undermined or overruled by your partner. Maybe you want a family member to take a look at their drinking and consider getting some help, yet these conversations lead to arguments. Maybe your input in decision-making never gets acknowledged. You get the picture.

I have seen all sorts of power struggles challenge families. Two areas it seems to show up in the most are parenting choices and custody battles. Family relationships can get quite contentious and messy when lawyers, grandparents, doctors, social workers, teachers, and other outside sources become involved in the mix. I remember being contacted by a mother who begged me to please help get her children back from her ex-husband. I let her know I would do everything I could but first I wanted to help her CLEANSE and clear the reactivity around the situation so that she would be able to see the best course of action and communicate with more composure, steadiness, and ease. It did not take long for her to realize how much her reactivity was interrupting, diverting, and even stalling the process. If you are feeling stuck, undermined, or disrespected, please spend some time with this CLEANSE.

Clear Reactivity I want you to close your eyes and imagine slowly gliding an ice cube over your face. See the ice in your mind, feel it slowly melting in your fingers as you touch your cheeks, forehead, and chin. Pause and breathe for thirty seconds before you proceed to step two.

Look Inward How I feel in my body right now is . . . inhale through your nose . . . exhale through your nose.

When I feel my thoughts, feelings, and intentions are not taken into account, it makes me feel . . . inhale . . . exhale . . .

When we butt heads or shut each other out, it makes me feel . . . inhale . . . exhale . . .

Having things escalate in this way makes me feel . . . inhale . . . exhale . . .

Emit Hum three times.

Activate See it! Visualize an image of relaxed attention and confidence. For example, maybe you see a peacock folding in his plumage or a deer contently nibbling on greenery.

Nourish Feel it! Notice how the peacock or the deer remain steady, alert yet fully present in the moment. How might you feel that in your body right now?

Surrender Say: "I allow release. I allow disarming. I allow alertness. I allow focused. I allow listening. I allow respect. I allow ease."

Ease Say: "I am feeling. I am respected. I am open. I am surrendering. I am breath. I am aware. I am comfort. I am ease."

Cleansing When a Family Member Is Struggling

Is someone you love struggling? Perhaps they are feeling depressed or overwhelmed by working through addiction. Maybe a family member has a chronic illness or had a recent health scare. Are you wondering what to do with an aging parent whose capabilities are diminishing, or an adult child who has recently lost their job, ended a relationship, or taken up some bad habits? This family member might even be you, and the pain you feel inside as memories of the past struggles surface. Or maybe you are feeling overwhelmed or burned out by the process of helping others. You most likely will want to do anything you can to help those family members or yourself, but before you do I encourage you to soften and surrender as you move through this CLEANSE and clear reactivity so you can see the emotions below the surface of the struggle.

180

Clear Reactivity Place your right hand on top of your left shoulder near your neck, tilt your right ear toward your right shoulder. As you do this squeeze your shoulder and give yourself a little massage. Then take your left hand to your right shoulder (again close to your neck) and squeeze. Bring your head back to center, relax your arms, and take in one deep inhale and release one clearing exhale before moving to step two.

Look Inward How I feel in my body right now is . . . inhale through your nose . . . exhale through your nose.

Coping with these problems and situations around me now makes me feel . . . inhale . . . exhale . . .

When I do not know what to do, it makes me feel . . . inhale . . . exhale . . .

When I think about what could happen, it makes me feel . . . inhale . . . exhale . . .

Emit Hum three times.

Activate See it! Visualize an image of boldness, bravery, fearlessness, grit, and strength. Perhaps an image of a warrior, a lioness, or a mountain.

Nourish Feel it! Imagine what it would feel like to be bold, brave, and fearless. How would it shift your gaze and your stance? Notice if you lift your chin or your body shifts. Sit in this energy for a moment.

Surrender Say: "I allow strength. I allow vulnerability. I allow resilience. I allow courage. I allow boldness. I allow fearlessness."

Ease Say: "I am fearless. I am strong. I am bold. I am brave. I am resilient."

Cleansing Codependent Behavior

Codependency happens in relationships, especially families, when one person supports or enables destructive or negative behavior like addiction, immaturity, acting out, irresponsibility, or even laziness. Among the core characteristics of most codependent people is a desperate need for approval to foster a sense of identity. This can manifest in doing things for people they can do for themselves, creating an environment that allows or at least doesn't discourage destructive habits, minimizing irresponsible behavior, or covering up things that ought to be addressed.

We often think our codependent behavior comes from a place of love and caring, but often it has the opposite result. Before you CLEANSE it is important to understand the difference between being supportive and being codependent. When you are helping or supporting another person, you both feel the benefits. For example, you might help your teenager apply for college—they are responsible for getting good grades and writing their essays while you look into financial aid. Each of you are doing your part and each of you will experience the benefits of doing so. Codependency is different; it can feel like one person is doing most of the work, the other person is doing less or staying stuck and somehow getting more. Another way you know if you are in a codependent relationship is if your life revolves around someone else. In other words, their wants, needs, desires come first all the time no matter what. A CLEANSE will help you get clear on what is really happening and illuminate how you can heal and begin to create healthy boundaries.

Clear Reactivity Tone your vagus nerve by imagining you are smelling the scent of lemon or lavender. Inhale through your nose as you take the fragrance in . . . then fully exhale through your nose. Pause for a moment.

Look Inward How I feel in my body right now is . . . inhale through your nose . . . exhale through your nose.

Having these strong emotions now makes me feel . . . inhale . . . exhale . . .

When I can't control what is happening, it makes me feel . . . inhale . . . exhale . . .

Surrendering this situation now makes me feel . . . inhale . . . exhale . . .

When I cling to the problem or person, it makes me feel . . . inhale . . . exhale . . .

Emit Hum three to six times with your mouth closed and your tongue pressed to the roof of your mouth.

Activate See it! Visualize an image of balance, nourishment, wholesomeness, and health. Perhaps a huge garden full of strawberries, squash, melons, tomatoes, and more.

Nourish Feel it! How would it feel to pick some of those fruits and vegetables right now? Taste the strawberries and savor their sweetness.

Surrender Say: "I allow purity. I allow naturalness. I allow detachment. I allow nourishment. I allow release. I allow wholesomeness. I allow health."

Ease Say: "I am healthy. I am balanced. I am secure. I am released. I am nourished. I am free."

Cleansing
Discipline

Discipline is about teaching and learning. The family unit is often the main place where we can expose our children to beliefs, behaviors, and the importance of cooperation and empathy. It's also where we practice and learn courteous and respectful communication and behavior as well as basic life skills like cooking, cleaning, and even laundry. If you are raising children you may at times feel undermined, ignored, or overruled by your partner or child when you attempt to establish rules or guidelines. Without some structure, chaos—both in terms of the family and our emotions—can ensue.

Perhaps you are a caregiver attempting to create routines and structure for your aging parents. Maybe you are realizing you need a bit more discipline yourself, because things were a bit loose when you were growing up and you feel you could benefit from some self-discipline. Things like going to bed early, getting off social media, increasing exercise, or laying off late-night snacks might help you create the stability, structure, and foundation you need to continue learning and growing. Whether it's a matter of finding the right energy around discipline for the people in your care or for yourself, this CLEANSE will help.

Clear Reactivity Stretch your mouth open wide and pause for a moment as you exercise the muscles in your face and jaw. Maybe even stick out and stretch your tongue. Repeat a few times until you feel you've released the tension you are holding in your face.

Look Inward How I feel in my body right now is . . . inhale through your nose . . . exhale through your nose.

When I create structure for myself it makes me feel . . . inhale . . . exhale . . .

When I try to discipline my mind and actions, it makes me feel . . . inhale . . . exhale . . .

When I think about the way I was disciplined, it makes me feel . . . inhale . . . exhale . . .

Emit Hum three times.

Activate See it! Visualize a healthy image of structure. A place you would go to learn, grow, and concentrate. Maybe you are listening to a public speaker you admire or being taught something you always wanted to learn like a musical instrument.

Nourish Feel it! Imagine the sensation in your body as you engage in learning about an interesting topic. How might you be sitting?

Surrender Say: "I allow learning. I allow growth. I allow engagement. I allow respect. I allow freedom."

Ease Say: "I am learning. I am growing. I am engaging. I am respected. I am free."

Cleansing Differences of Opinion

Has there been a rift in your family? Perhaps you are no longer speaking to one of your relatives after an argument or maybe your teenager is giving you the cold shoulder and won't let go of their anger after you enforced consequences for misbehavior. Although quite a bit of time may have passed, the tension between you may not have diminished. When it comes to families, I have heard quite a few stories about how people manage their upset feelings by shutting down or with passive-aggressive behavior, such as withholding love, money, affection, communication, or connection. When reactions such as these set in, they can leave you feeling a bit angry, confused, or hurt. You may wish it could be a better situation and think, "If only they would apologize, see things from my point of view, chill out, and listen to my side." Before you settle on the best way to mend fences, know that rather than linger in the past it will help to take some time to consider the emotions underlying your side of the disagreement by doing this CLEANSE.

Clear Reactivity Bring your arms to your sides and make fists with each of your hands. Hold the squeeze for three seconds and then release your fingers. Inhale . . . exhale . . . and then squeeze again. Repeat this sequence two more times before you move to step two.

Look Inward How I feel in my body right now is . . . inhale through your nose . . . exhale through your nose.

When I hold on to past conversations, interactions, events, and silences, it makes me feel . . . inhale . . . exhale . . .

Releasing the energy around these situations now makes me feel . . . inhale . . . exhale . . .

Emit Hum three times.

Activate See it! Visualize an image of harmony, love, forgiveness. Imagine what it would look like in nature. Perhaps the way a tree might branch at different angles, yet it remains one whole tree.

Nourish Feel it! Breathe into your visualization, smell the sap of your tree, sense the ground under your feet, hear the rustle of leaves above you.

Surrender Say: "I allow love. I allow harmony. I allow peace. I allow forgiveness. I allow freedom."

Ease Say: "I am love. I am harmony. I am at peace. I am forgiveness. I am free."

Part IV

WORK & COMMUNITY

When we **process our emotions** related to the world beyond family and home, we can improve our daily lives and society as a whole.

As I wrote this book, the world was facing a devastating public health and economic crisis due to the coronavirus pandemic. This impacted and continues to impact not just people's physical health, but their mental health at a magnitude we can't yet quantify. It seemed like everyone around me was filing for unemployment. Within three weeks, two of my sisters-in-law, my oldest daughter, and several of my students had lost their jobs. My husband's company announced they could keep everyone full-time for about a month, and to save my business, I had to develop an entirely new teaching model including online group CLEANSEs so I could keep costs down.

At the same time, human compassion reached an all-time high. Communities united as people consoled those who had lost loved ones, tended to the sick, and made sure everyone was safe and had enough to eat. The message spread—check in with each other, help out, and stay strong. It seemed like overnight, parents (many of them newly working from home) became teachers, adding homeschooling to their daily tasks.

As you can imagine, reactivity and mental health awareness were also at an all-time high. Then, in June 2020, the National Alliance on Mental Illness came out with the following recommendations[2] for promoting mental health in the workplace:

- **Dedicate company resources to supporting workplace mental health.**

- **Recognize that family challenges may impact mental health by developing policies to promote better work-life balance.**

- **Foster a culture where seeking help is a sign of strength.**

- **Reject and prohibit stigma.**

- **Encourage open and honest discussions with employees about mental health issues, including anonymous feedback on workplace policies.**

It felt as if the entire world were going through a collective CLEANSE of some sort. While these situations have occurred before in our history, what has been different this time is how technology was able to keep us interconnected. However, the one thing technology cannot replace is the intelligence of our emotions and how they can help move us in a more secure, solid, healthy, and stable direction, enhancing our physical and mental well-being when we choose to process them. In the past, work and home were like two separate entities. Now with many people working from home, emotional reactivity in the home can more easily carry over at work and vice versa. The good news is when you detox some of the triggers (reactions) in your personal life, this will positively spill into your professional life.

Cleansing Fear of Conflict

Fear of conflict was a hot topic one Monday evening. That is the night I teach a three-hour Psychology 101 class to students of all ages, backgrounds, and abilities at a local community college. Since most of my students work and go to school, discussions about conflict in the workplace are quite common. Yes, I heard it all that evening: people feeling undermined, unsupported, and frustrated with the behaviors and attitudes of their coworkers and bosses. Some of the students were hoping to quit their jobs once they earned their degrees, while others wanted to know more about how to deal with difficult customers, colleagues, and employees in the future.

I know they're not alone. How many of us have dreaded making waves in the workplace or opening an email from a combative manager or coworker? How often has it held you back from doing a good job and advancing in your career? Here you get to move through the entire process.

Clear Reactivity Blow air through your closed lips and make a buzzing sound, kind of like a bumblebee. What this does is encourage you to have a long, deliberate exhale. Inhale, and repeat this buzzing three times in a row.

Look Inward How I feel in my body right now is . . . inhale through your nose . . . exhale through your nose.

When customers, my boss, or clients get upset, it makes me feel . . . inhale . . . exhale . . .

Managing these situations makes me feel . . . inhale . . . exhale . . .

Being present for myself right now makes me feel . . . inhale . . . exhale . . .

Emit Hum three times.

Activate See it! Visualize an image of stillness, quiet, calm, restoration, and support. Perhaps lily pads floating on a dark green pond.

Nourish Feel it! Imagine being as calm and quiet as those lily pads, rooted in stillness and restoration.

Surrender Say: "I allow restoration. I allow support. I allow calm. I allow comfort. I allow ease."

Ease Say: "I am ease. I am restoration. I am rejuvenation. I am comfort. I am calm."

Cleansing Competition

Competition can be a wonderful way to get people motivated. Throw a little reward—maybe extra vacation time, a cash bonus, bragging rights, or a promotion—into the mix and you just might energize your team. Yet when competition goes too far, fame, greed, and hunger for power can take over and lead to underhanded or unethical behaviors, stress, or more attention to winning than cooperation among coworkers. As a result, people lose faith in the process, may get hurt, and or give up altogether because they don't see themselves as winning, so why bother at all?

If you are in a situation where you feel competition is obscuring collaboration, or perhaps you have a hunch there may be some cheating or favoritism involved, consider taking this opportunity to CLEANSE. On the other hand, if you are feeling like your team is a bit complacent, you wish people would challenge each other more, this CLEANSE will help with that as well.

Clear Reactivity Swish your tongue around in the saliva in your mouth. (I know it's kind of gross, but it works.) Do this for about twenty seconds before you proceed to step two.

Look Inward How I feel in my body right now is . . . inhale through your nose . . . exhale through your nose.

When the expectations are too high, it makes me feel . . . inhale . . . exhale . . .

Seeing others reach their goal makes me feel . . . inhale . . . exhale . . .

When things seem aggressive or unfair, it makes me feel . . . inhale . . . exhale . . .

Emit Hum three times.

Activate See it! Visualize an image of imperfection. Perhaps a tree in midwinter or a worn book.

Nourish Feel it! Imagine what it would feel like to hold that book or sit by a tree with bare branches. Touch the bark, feel the texture in your hands now.

Surrender Say: "I allow imperfection. I allow growth. I allow peace. I allow effort. I allow non-effort."

Ease Say: "I am effort. I am non-effort. I am motivated. I am centered. I am victorious. I am free."

Cleansing Lack of Enthusiasm

You may encounter times when your job feels dull, robotic, or un-stimulating. Sure it pays the bills, but you don't feel as fulfilled as you once did. You wish you could find something with equal or better pay, work that felt a bit more meaningful and closer to who you are and what you value. What once seemed like a good fit has changed and as a result you just don't arrive at your desk with the same positive verve. You feel heavy, frustrated, and stuck. And if everyone at your workplaces seems to be miserable or disagreeable, perhaps you are not alone. What I have found is sometimes groups of people are attempting to CLEANSE shared reactions. In other words, you are all having similar feelings because of a situation but they are manifesting as different reactions. Before you quit your job, I suggest you let go of analysis for a moment and take some time to CLEANSE.

Clear Reactivity Tone your vagus nerve by singing. Yes, singing. It can be a classic like "Row, Row, Row Your Boat," your favorite song on the radio, or simply a few bars of "la, la, la." Whatever you choose, sing for at least twenty seconds.

Look Inward How I feel in my body right now is . . . inhale through your nose . . . exhale through your nose.

When things get boring or repetitive, it makes me feel . . . inhale . . . exhale . . .

Having these thoughts now about my job makes me feel . . . inhale . . . exhale . . .

Being in this situation now makes me feel . . . inhale . . . exhale . . .

Emit Hum three times.

Activate See it! Visualize an image of anticipation, eagerness, or passion. Perhaps what it would feel like to wait for something you love—like a concert or a baseball game or a delicious meal—to begin.

Nourish Feel it! Imagine what it would feel to be in that state of joyful anticipation. How does enthusiasm feel in your body? Do you have butterflies in your stomach?

Surrender Say: "I allow freshness. I allow fun. I allow new. I allow laughter. I allow connection."

Ease Say: "I am fresh. I am enthusiastic. I am growing. I am fun. I am laughter."

Cleansing
Rudeness

If you have a job in customer service, such as in a restaurant or in the accounts receivable department of a business, it is likely you have come across some rude behavior. To help you get clear on what you are going to CLEANSE, let me remind you of what rude looks like. I say this because sometimes people get so used to being on the receiving end of rudeness they become desensitized and forget what it is like to be treated with courtesy and respect!

It is not rude to speak up, voice your opinion, ask questions, or let someone know you are disappointed or unhappy. Rudeness is when someone uses a sharp tone or engages in disrespectful, diminishing, or offensive behavior. For example, they might be pushy and cut you off in line, complain loudly so everyone else can hear what they think of you, bark a reply, or not reply at all. Rudeness can also occur when someone treats you as if you don't exist at all. For example, they might talk on their phone while cashing out at the grocery store, never acknowledging you as a person who is assisting them. Now that we are clear, let's CLEANSE.

Clear Reactivity Stretch your arms overhead as you inhale through your nose and squeeze your fingers together into two fists. Hold the squeeze for five seconds and then on the exhale release your arms and let them drop to your sides while unclenching your fingers. Repeat two or three times before you move to step two.

Look Inward How I feel in my body right now is . . . inhale through your nose . . . exhale through your nose.

When this person treated me in this way, it made me feel . . . inhale . . . exhale . . .

Holding back my true feelings in these situations makes me feel . . . inhale . . . exhale . . .

Emit Hum three times.

Activate See it! Visualize an image of kindness, gentleness, courtesy, and respect. Perhaps someone holding the door open for you or wiping their feet before entering your home.

Nourish Feel it! Imagine wiping your feet off on a mat right now. What sensations do you feel on the soles of your shoes?

Surrender Say: "I allow kindness. I allow gentleness. I allow courtesy. I allow respect."

Ease Say: "I am kind. I am gentle. I am compassionate. I am forgiving. I am love."

Cleansing Unemployment or Being Laid Off

According to Jeanne Meister in *Forbes* magazine in 2012, "The average worker today stays at each of his or her jobs for 4.4 years, according to the most recent available data from the Bureau of Labor Statistics."[3] I imagine the numbers are even lower now. This is quite different from the days when keeping the same job or staying with a company for twenty or thirty years was expected. It is always a sad day when companies go under and good people lose their source of income. While losing or quitting a job can create an opportunity for something new and possibly better to come into your life, if you have unprocessed emotions such as fear, rejection, hurt, anger, or frustration, you run the risk of missing what they can teach you. Un-processed emotions, especially ones of powerlessness, can leave you feeling exhausted, doubtful, and confused. So if you are looking to find or attract something new or even make the most of an unstable work situation, I suggest you begin with a CLEANSE.

Clear Reactivity Tone the vagus nerve by using a hand mudra. Like most mudras, if you hold it for a minute or two while breathing in and out through your nose you will help move the emotional energy in your body, increasing power of your breath. This time make the "okay" sign by pressing the tips of your pointer and thumb together while leaving the other fingers loose. Hold this for thirty seconds or so until you feel yourself engage with your breath.

Look Inward How I feel in my body right now is . . . inhale through your nose . . . exhale through your nose.

Being in this situation makes me feel . . . inhale . . . exhale . . .

When I am unsure of the future I feel . . . inhale . . . exhale . . .

Looking for a new job or hoping to get rehired in the future makes me feel . . . inhale . . . exhale . . .

Emit Hum three times.

Activate See it! Visualize an image of trust. For example, the sun— you can pretty much trust it is on the other side of those clouds.

Nourish Feel it! Imagine feeling the sun emerge through a gray sky, see the way the light would change, how it might shift the atmosphere.

Surrender Say: "I allow trust. I allow ease. I allow change. I allow new beginnings. I allow completion. I allow freedom."

Ease Say: "I am new beginnings. I am endings. I am change. I am transformation. I am free."

200

Cleansing Fear of Public Speaking

Public speaking can be a terrifying experience. Whether it is getting up in front of a group of people at a meeting, teaching a class, or presenting a live event on social media, public speaking can quickly bring up fear, feelings of low self-worth, and anxiety that (without a CLEANSE) can be difficult to move through. If you are afraid to speak in public know you are not alone, it's a phobia that is quite common—about 25 percent of people report having it.[4] However, before you avoid the chance to share your message, story, or insight with others consider this may be an opportunity for you to CLEANSE fear of being evaluated, judged, or criticized. You might have a bit of a physical reaction like a blotchy neck, heavy perspiration, or jittery hands, but think of this as feedback that your body is open, energized, and ready to move through whatever is rising up in the moment.

Clear Reactivity Do a few standing squats with your feet hip-width apart. Bend at your knees like you are sitting in a chair and then stand up straight. Go as far down as feels comfortable and do this at your own pace. Repeat two or three times in a row.

Look Inward How I feel in my body right now is . . . inhale through your nose . . . exhale through your nose.

When I think of everyone staring at me, it makes me feel . . . inhale . . . exhale . . .

Having others listen to me speak aloud makes me feel . . . inhale . . . exhale . . .

The thought of messing up or failing in public makes me feel . . . inhale . . . exhale . . .

Emit Hum three times.

Activate See it! Visualize an image of praise, approval, respect, and confidence. Maybe it's appreciative applause from a group of trusted colleagues or a letter of recommendation.

Nourish Feel it! Imagine receiving praise, applause, compliments, and gratitude. How would it feel in your body? You might be warm, happy, and excited inside.

Surrender Say: "I allow calm. I allow focus. I allow clarity. I allow praise. I allow worthy. I allow confidence."

Ease Say: "I am calm. I am focused. I am praised. I am worthy. I am victorious."

Cleansing Chaos

Have you ever had a work experience that left you feeling completely overwhelmed by chaos? Perhaps your boss dumped a million tasks on your desk without giving you a sense of what the priorities were. Perhaps a series of layoffs have left the remaining members of your team wondering exactly what their responsibilities were. Maybe your computer crashed right before you had a big project due, half the staff called in sick during a busy period, or a team member's behavior has become unreliable.

Part of you might get a little rush from the chaos, because let's face it, chaos does make things a little bit more interesting and the day goes faster . . . sometimes too fast. Yet another part of you might feel overwhelmed, not even know where to start, and want to give up and quit altogether. This can happen even if you've had some experience in dealing with chaos, like if you are a healthcare provider who is used to a rather erratic workflow. No matter where you land on the spectrum, when left uncleansed, the feeling of everything being thrown at you at once and struggling to catch your breath can lead to problems at work and in life. So if you have had a chaotic day, week, month, or know you're about to have one, this is a CLEANSE you will want to come back to regularly.

Clear Reactivity This mudra is an effortless way to bring calming energy into your body. Bring the tips of your thumbs, middle fingers, and ring fingers together on each hand, allowing the other fingers to remain straight. Rest your hands palms-up on your lap for thirty seconds. Inhale . . . exhale deliberately and fully before you move on to step two.

Look Inward How I feel in my body right now is . . . inhale through your nose . . . exhale through your nose.

When things happen unexpectedly, it makes me feel . . . inhale . . . exhale . . .

When things get chaotic and overwhelming, it makes me feel . . . inhale . . . exhale . . .

Emit Hum three times.

Activate See it! Visualize an image of calm, reassurance, certainty, and relaxation. Perhaps an image of a sturdy oak tree or vast cornfields.

Nourish Feel it! Imagine what it would feel like in this reassuring setting. Perhaps a sense of grounding where you can notice the way your feet connect with the earth.

Surrender Say: "I allow grounding. I allow reassurance. I allow certainty. I allow faith. I allow calm."

Ease Say: "I am calm. I am stable. I am supported. I am trusting. I am faith."

Cleansing When a Coworker Rubs You the Wrong Way

Sometimes you get lucky and work in an environment where everyone gets along and supports one another, but often there are one or two people who rub you the wrong way and can really get under your skin! Before you think about all the reasons that person annoys you—their inflated ego, laziness, negativity, or propensity for gossip—know that dwelling on their behavior may actually be fueling rather than processing your own strong emotions. You see, as difficult as it may be, what irritates you about that person is somehow connected to a reactive pattern within yourself. Otherwise you would not get so triggered. Know by spending a few minutes with this CLEANSE now and as needed, you will release and eventually dissolve what is showing up in you to be healed. As your re-activity is revealed and healed, it's likely the situation with your coworker will change for the better, and even if it doesn't, your reactions will!

Clear Reactivity Sit up nice and tall with both feet flat on the floor, hip-width apart. Take your right hand and place it on top of your left shoulder as you tilt your head toward the right for a neck stretch. Be sure to hold the stretch for a minimum of three counts as this helps you get deeper. Repeat on the other side, taking your left hand, and placing it on top of your right shoulder as you tilt your left ear, toward the left shoulder. Return to center and take moment to absorb your breath before you continue.

Look Inward How I feel in my body right now is . . . inhale through your nose . . . exhale through your nose.

Being around or interacting with this person makes me feel . . . inhale . . . exhale . . .

When I am around this person, they remind me of . . . inhale . . . exhale . . .

Coping with this situation makes me feel . . . inhale . . . exhale . . .

Emit Hum three times.

Activate See it! Visualize images of friendliness, hospitality, and approachability. Perhaps an image of a dog wagging its tail in greeting or a cat a rubbing against your leg.

Nourish Feel it! Feel in your body what it would be like to be around a friendly animal. How might it open your heart and get you to soften your stance?

Surrender Say: "I allow calm. I allow release. I allow contentment. I allow pleasure."

Ease Say: "I am calm. I am happy. I am warm. I am content. I am at peace."

Cleansing Feeling Trapped

Do you feel trapped or caught in a situation at work you just can't get out of? Perhaps you have been waiting to be moved to a new shift or promoted into a different position. Maybe you are looking to change careers altogether. Maybe you're ready to retire but can't afford to. Perhaps you signed a contract or agreed to partner with someone with whom you no longer wish to work.

Without a CLEANSE, the feeling of being trapped can lead to difficulties expressing yourself clearly. For example, you may hear yourself saying one thing while on the inside believing something quite different. It is like nodding your head, smiling in agreement while holding back that word "No!" you really want to blurt. You tell yourself you can't because you could upset that person, cause a rift, or jeopardize all your efforts to change your position. Take a breath, slow down; this is a sign you are moving into reactivity and need to CLEANSE. Once you do, you'll likely see your way out of the situation.

Clear Reactivity Find a comfortable seated position away from distractions, and allow yourself to sit in silence for about a minute. As you do, observe your body and breathe. Inhale . . . exhale . . . and now open your eyes, pause for one more breath.

Look Inward How I feel in my body right now is . . . inhale through your nose . . . exhale through your nose.

When I feel I do not have a choice, it makes me feel . . . inhale . . . exhale . . .

Opening my mind to other possibilities makes me feel . . . inhale . . . exhale . . .

When I do not know what else to do I feel . . . inhale . . . exhale . . .

Emit Hum three times.

Activate See it! Visualize an image of openness, possibilities, and choice. Perhaps an image of two paths diverging in a beautiful green forest. See them as enticing, picturesque, and grounding.

Nourish Feel it! Allow yourself to pause and imagine the feeling in your body. How does it feel when you allow yourself to explore the forest? How does it feel when you commit to taking one of the paths?

Surrender Say: "I allow movement. I allow exploration. I allow curiosity. I allow freedom. I allow choice."

Ease Say: "I am choice. I am in motion. I am exploring. I am journeying. I am change."

Cleansing People-Pleasing

Seen from the outside, people-pleasing is when you go along with something out of fear of being judged or making waves. For example, you might stay at the after-work party because you do not want to appear like a bore or a party pooper. You might accept tasks that aren't yours to do because it's easier than standing up for yourself. I have chosen to place people-pleasing in the work and community section yet I often find it can cross over into home life, family, and even health. It's a way so many of us bury or avoid our emotions!

After moving through this CLEANSE with many clients, I have learned people-pleasing is a reaction; a way to manage strong feelings of guilt and fear. In addition, there are quite a few beliefs that often accompany this pattern. Ones such as, "If I don't say yes, I will be viewed as difficult and people won't like me," "I might not be included in the future if I don't give in now," or "This would mean that somehow I am a failure and not part of the team." As you can see, people-pleasing runs deep, which is why it is such an important issue to CLEANSE.

Clear Reactivity As you press on the roof of your mouth with your tongue, sweep it from back to front and front to back three to five times. Notice how saliva increases in your mouth. Pause, swallow, and create space for one or two slow, deep breaths. Take your time as you . . . inhale . . . exhale . . . and move to step two.

Look Inward How I feel in my body right now is . . . inhale through your nose . . . exhale through your nose.

When I say no, it makes me feel . . . inhale . . . exhale . . .

Saying yes makes me feel . . . inhale . . . exhale . . .

Recognizing these thoughts and fears right now makes me feel . . . inhale . . . exhale.

Emit Hum three times.

Activate See it! Visualize an image of energy—sparkly, shimmery light bouncing on the water or across the sky.

Nourish Feel it! Imagine taking in that energy as you relax and nourish your body. Notice the way it feels to close your eyes, slow down, and savor the moment.

Surrender Say: "I allow presence. I allow consciousness. I allow energy. I allow vibration. I allow ease."

Ease Say: "I am present. I am energy. I am nourished. I am connected. I am whole. I am free."

Cleansing for Boundaries

Boundaries come in all shapes and sizes. Some are more physical in nature, like walls to create space and privacy. Other boundaries are about supporting your emotional needs. When it comes to the workplace you may be looking for more personal space, perhaps a few minutes between tasks, a moment to eat your lunch, or for your colleagues and coworkers to be mindful to not text or call you late at night or when you are on vacation. Right now, you may feel as if you are the only one who can manage a work situation, that you're indispensable, and therefore, you allow this behavior to continue. Boundaries are about showing other people how to behave, and sometimes that means providing them with the skills and coaching so they can handle things on their own, but before you can do that you need to know what your own boundaries are.

There are also situations where a coworker might be getting a little too close. Perhaps they are flirty, text you after work, or tell you a little too much about their personal life. If you are having trouble letting this person know they have gone a little too far, take some time to CLEANSE, so you can gain the strength and wherewithal to be clear about what you will and will not tolerate.

Clear Reactivity Tilt your right ear toward your right shoulder. Take your right hand, and gently press the left side of your head as you continue to stretch your neck for about thirty seconds or so. Move your head back to center and tilt it to the left. This time take your left hand and cup your right ear as you gently stretch your neck. Bring your head back to center and observe your breath for one inhale . . . and exhale . . . before you move to step two.

Look Inward How I feel in my body right now is . . . inhale through your nose . . . exhale through your nose.

When someone oversteps the boundaries around me, it makes me feel . . . inhale . . . exhale . . .

When I am having difficulty creating boundaries within myself, I notice I am feeling . . . inhale . . . exhale . . .

Having this person overstep the boundaries now makes me feel . . . inhale . . . exhale . . .

Emit Hum three times.

Activate See it! Visualize looking out across a horizon—maybe the ocean—that stretches farther than the eye can see.

Nourish Feel it! Imagine comfort, space, quiet, expanse, and calm. How does this feel in your body?

Surrender Say: "I allow comfort. I allow soothing. I allow quiet. I allow space. I allow assertiveness. I allow my needs. I allow desire."

Ease Say: "I am comfort. I am spacious. I am expansive. I am assertive. I am quiet. I am soothed."

212

Cleansing Drama

Drama happens whenever a situation or story gets out of hand. As it spreads from one person to the next, the energy gets a little stronger and a little thicker. You can identify drama by the little extra bite it brings to a situation. A hand on the hip, secretive conversations in the corner, or a look of paranoia or blankness on people's faces when you ask them what's up. It can also be identified by impulsive behavior, someone suddenly announcing they are going to quit or tossing out an f-bomb during a meeting. Drama can also look like arguing, lots of complaining, or individuals refusing to speak to one another. When a group is overcome by a dramatic situation you're often expected to take sides whether you want to or not.

Drama impacts us all at one time or another and fuels anxiety as well tightness and even congestion in our bodies. To avoid getting caught up in drama or to extricate yourself from one, take a moment now and CLEANSE.

Clear Reactivity Interlace your fingers behind your head as you sit up tall, keeping your arms bent, elbows out to the side. Gently turn your head to the right as you look toward your right elbow, and then to the left as you look toward your left elbow. Move your hands to your hips, and again turn your head gently to the right and then swipe your chin over to the left. Drop your arms down to your sides as you turn your head to the right and left one more time. Release and breathe.

Look Inward How I feel in my body right now is . . . inhale through your nose . . . exhale through your nose.

When things get intense or heated, it makes me feel . . . inhale . . . exhale . . .

When I get caught up in reactivity, it makes me feel . . . inhale . . . exhale . . .

Emit Hum three times.

Activate See it! Visualize an image of peace, calm, sweetness, and neutrality. Perhaps a glass of milk or a bowl of vanilla ice cream. (You can pick your flavor, but vanilla always makes me feel neutral.)

Nourish Feel it! Imagine holding the bowl of ice cream in your hands before you taste it. How does it feel? How do you feel?

Surrender Say: "I allow cooling. I allow transformation. I allow merging. I allow dissolving. I allow neutralizing."

Ease Say: "I am cooling. I am transforming. I am dissolving. I am healing. I am neutralizing."

Cleansing
Disagreements

Disagreements happen, even in the workplace. There will always be times when people have difficulties seeing eye to eye and power struggles will ensue. Often these include bickering or misunderstandings. I remember my dentist and his technician having a little tiff right in front of me over dental floss while I was in the chair, my mouth wide open. It was one of those, *I said/no you said* situations. When the dentist looked away the technician rolled her eyes at me. Some disagreements are harmless like this one but are perhaps a sign that individuals are having a bad day. Others can become quite dangerous and create a toxic work environment. Left unresolved or unattended to, disagreements can pollute an entire workplace or community with negativity. Suddenly people start to feel annoyed, disrespected, and blatantly reactive. Before things get out of hand or if you need to recover, try this CLEANSE.

Clear Reactivity Take a moment now and clear the air by sitting up tall with both feet flat on the floor. Open your arms wide and then cross them in front of you. Pause. Open your arms up wide again and cross them in front again with the opposite arm on top this time. Think of the gesture like the way an umpire makes a call in a baseball game. Repeat this sequence three times and don't forget to breathe!

Look Inward How I feel in my body right now is . . . inhale through your nose . . . exhale through your nose.

Holding on to negative energy makes me feel . . . inhale . . . exhale . . .

Clearing the air in this way makes me feel . . . inhale . . . exhale . . .

Loosening this energy now makes me feel . . . inhale . . . exhale . . .

Emit Hum three times.

Activate See it! Visualize an image of cohesiveness. Perhaps the experience of placing the last few pieces to complete a jigsaw puzzle. What makes you feel calm and whole?

Nourish Feel it! Imagine what it would feel like in your body right now to be whole, complete, with no forces pushing against you. Would you feel grounded?

Surrender Say: "I allow understanding. I allow softening. I allow listening. I allow resolution. I allow inclusion. I allow whole."

Ease Say: "I am resolution. I am understanding. I am softening. I am enough. I am whole. I am free."

Cleansing Work Itself

"Can you give me a CLEANSE to do after work?"

People ask me this all the time! Now with smartphones and computers work travels with you wherever you go. And this is even more the case now that so many people are working from home. It can be so easy and tempting to respond to an email, text message, or phone call after hours, in the car on the way home, at the gym, or while you are having dinner.

So often, without a CLEANSE, it can feel like you have a ton of loose ends. In other words, you never really gain the calming feeling of completion. Since so many jobs today allow you to work around the clock, the old ways of wrapping up a task are kind of over. Now it is about cultivating a feeling of completion from within. This means taking a moment to CLEANSE either in between tasks, during breaks, or at the end of your day or shift.

Clear Reactivity Rub the palms of your hands together for twenty seconds as you create some heat from the friction. Take your dominant hand and place it on the upper part of your neck at the base of your skull. Enjoy some nice deep breaths as you inhale through your nose . . . and exhale through your nose.

Look Inward How I feel in my body right now is . . . inhale through your nose . . . exhale through your nose.

Having work on my mind makes me feel . . . inhale . . . exhale . . .

Walking away or taking a break right now makes me feel . . . inhale . . . exhale . . .

When there is still more work to do, it makes me feel . . . inhale . . . exhale . . .

Emit Hum three times.

Activate See it! Visualize an image of release, of letting go. Perhaps you are sinking into a lovely, fragrant, warm bubble bath.

Nourish Feel it! Notice how being in the tub or even just soaking your feet in water would relax your muscles. Release.

Surrender Say: "I allow release. I allow letting go. I allow softening. I allow dissolving. I allow presence."

Ease Say: "I am softening. I am present. I am releasing. I am balanced. I am free."

Cleansing Making a Decision

So you have a decision to make. Perhaps you are wondering whether to hire someone, speak up about a problem at work, or cut someone's hours. Maybe you have constructive feedback to give to a coworker or you are deciding whether to cancel an appointment or attend a company gathering. Maybe you've been offered a new job but aren't sure about making the transition. Before you weigh out the pros and cons, let's gather some energy around the situation by taking a moment to CLEANSE. You see, what I have learned is if you feel like you are getting stuck in the process and are not sure what to do, it's likely you are not focusing on the decision at all, but instead are focusing on the outcome. Make sense?

In this practice, I encourage you to put a little extra something into the Nourish step as you take an extra moment to breathe.

Clear Reactivity Sit up tall and place both feet flat on the floor. Lift your right foot a few inches and extend your leg out in front of you while the other foot remains on the floor. Hold your leg out straight for one . . . two . . . three . . . seconds. Release, pause, breathe, and repeat on the other side.

Look Inward How I feel in my body right now is . . . inhale through your nose . . . exhale through your nose.

When I attach to outcome, it makes me feel . . . inhale . . . exhale . . .

When I worry about what may or may not happen, it makes me feel . . . inhale . . . exhale . . .

Emit Hum three times.

Activate See it! Visualize an image of strength, confidence, assertiveness, and calm. For me, the image of a giraffe comes to mind as it regally looks toward the horizon, observing the whole scene, and seems to know exactly when to take another step.

Nourish Feel it! Put a little extra breath in here today. Fill up your abdomen on the inhale like a balloon for the count of one . . . two . . . three. Hold for a count of one . . . two . . . and release your abdomen for a count of one . . . two . . . three . . . as you pull your navel toward your spine.

Surrender Say: "I allow process. I allow focus. I allow pause. I allow presence. I allow calm. I allow assertiveness. I allow transformation."

Ease Say: "I am process. I am present. I am calm. I am pausing. I am transformation. I am choice. I am heard. I am free."

Cleansing Uncertainty

Are you concerned about your security? Perhaps you are wondering if the position or job you are in is solid or stable? Maybe you're worried about what will happen when your unemployment benefits end? Either way, you may be feeling uncertain or fearful about the future. Here is the thing about uncertainty, if left unattended it can make you feel like you are trapped on shaky ground and, as a result, you may find yourself looking for something to hold on to. The challenge is the more you try to hold on—to a job, an idea—the more resistance you create. There is likely a real opportunity for you at this time in your life, and while most of us like to have an idea of what lies on the other side before we even consider letting go, as you might have already realized, we don't always have that luxury. This is a time for surrender, and may this CLEANSE gently guide you through.

Clear Reactivity Take a moment now and drink some water. These kinds of stressors can dehydrate you. Go ahead fill a glass with icy water and take some sips.

Look Inward How I feel in my body right now is . . . inhale through your nose . . . exhale through your nose.

When I am not sure what lies ahead, it makes me feel . . . inhale . . . exhale . . .

Sitting in this space of uncertainty now makes me feel . . . inhale . . . exhale . . .

When I wonder what to do, it makes me feel . . . inhale . . . exhale . . .

Emit Hum three times.

Activate See it! Visualize an image of certainty, surrender, detachment, freedom, and curiosity. It can be as simple as picturing yourself unlocking a door and allowing it to open wide.

Nourish Feel it! Imagine standing in front of that doorway now, sun on your face, a fresh breeze blowing in.

Surrender Say: "I allow movement. I allow growth. I allow expansion. I allow unrestricting. I allow curiosity. I allow faith. I allow freedom."

Ease Say: "I am faith. I am curious. I am open. I am willing. I am trusting. I am free."

Cleansing Working Overtime

Are you balancing two jobs, covering someone else's shift, burning the midnight oil to meet a deadline, or doing your best to be a parent and maybe a homeschooling teacher while working at the same time? These are examples of what working overtime looks like. It can be anything you do in addition to your daily tasks and responsibilities. It may include traveling on a business trip, emailing and taking phone calls from home, or coming in on weekends. While technology has made some things easier, it also has contributed to blurring the lines between being on and off the clock and if you are a parent or caretaker, you may not get the luxury of thinking in those terms.

Here is the thing, the days of punching a time clock are pretty much over, so rather than try to measure your workload in hours and minutes, I suggest you develop the skill of checking in with yourself. Ask yourself, "How am I feeling today?" Instead of answering that question immediately, take some time to just breathe. Let your breath answer just like you do in each CLEANSE. There might be some days when you are fine with taking on a lot of responsibilities and tasks and others when it all becomes too much. Also, allowing oneself to be in a place of feeling constantly overwhelmed can be a way of running away from emotions you need to process.

Clear Reactivity Interlace your fingers, turn your palms outward, and stretch your arms up and over your head. Relax your shoulders and stretch side to side. As you do this, release a nice, wide yawn. Repeat two or three more times.

Look Inward How I feel in my body right now is . . . inhale through your nose . . . exhale through your nose.

When I have little time for myself, it makes me feel . . . inhale . . . exhale . . .

When work takes over my life, it makes me feel . . . inhale . . . exhale . . .

Overextending myself in this way makes me feel . . . inhale . . . exhale . . .

Emit Hum three times.

Activate See it! Visualize an image of rest, calm, solitude, peace, and centeredness. Perhaps the feeling of sitting in a lounge chair overlooking a lake.

Nourish Feel it! Imagine what it would feel like to be in a place where you could take in the world around you. The beach, fields, mountains, breathe in the air.

Surrender Say: "I allow space. I allow sensations. I allow ease. I allow being."

Ease Say: "I am being. I am breath. I am sensing. I am releasing. I am centering. I am free."

Cleansing When Someone Does Not Give You Credit for Your Ideas

Creativity is at the heart of innovation, connection, and vision and it's often a very personal thing. Ideas in the workplace can shift the course of long-range projections, increase sales, or foster community. They are like gold. However, if you share your ideas and someone else takes them or treats them as if they were their own, this can leave you feeling angry, resentful, and hopeless. As a result, motivation, trust, and collaboration are likely to dwindle, that is unless you take the time to CLEANSE. So if you were someone who offered an idea, or maybe contributed to solving a problem and did not receive any recognition or credit, now is your time to CLEANSE the ways you may have suppressed the emotions around these kinds of circumstances.

Clear Reactivity Rub the palms of your hands together vigorously for twenty seconds. Place your palms on your forehead one on top of the other as you breathe in . . . and breathe out . . . through your nose. Hold your hands on your forehead for twenty more seconds.

Look Inward How I feel in my body right now is . . . inhale through your nose . . . exhale through your nose.

When I did not receive credit for my work, ideas, or contribution, it made me feel . . . inhale . . . exhale . . .

When I realized this was happening, it made me feel . . . inhale . . . exhale . . .

Emit Hum three times.

Activate See it! Visualize an image of recognition, order, honor, respect, and credibility. Perhaps a bouquet of flowers or a gold medal.

Nourish Feel it! Smell the bouquet, hold the medal in your hands. Imagine how you lift your head as you accept the honor.

Surrender Say: "I allow order. I allow recognition. I allow clarity. I allow transparency. I allow honor. I allow respect."

Ease Say: "I am ordered. I am honored. I am respected. I am confident. I am credible. I am worthy."

Cleansing Disorganization

Do you have stacks of papers on your desk? Is your inbox full of old emails? Or maybe you are behind on writing a blog, updating your website, sending out invoices, or following up with team members or customers. Maybe you are a student with loads of assignments and deadlines, attempting to balance classwork with your job's schedule. Ask yourself, "How does it make me feel when I am disorganized?" Does it make you feel frustrated, anxious, and overwhelmed? As a result, how does this impact your work performance? Are you forgetting appointments, losing track of things, or maybe constantly feeling rushed, unable to really be present? If so, remember it happens to everyone—we all get jumbled or need to find a clear path through our tasks—so before you begin putting yourself back in order by making a list, cleaning your desk, or replying to those emails I suggest you CLEANSE.

Clear Reactivity If you are able, get down on the floor onto a soft surface like a rug or yoga mat. Move into a tabletop position with your hands directly under your shoulders, your knees under your hips. Do a few cat-cow stretches as you inhale and lift your head, heart, and tailbone toward the ceiling. On the exhale, round your spine as you tuck in your chin and tailbone. Repeat this sequence, arching up and down two or three times in a row. (If you prefer you can also do this while seated in a chair. As you inhale, open your chest, lift your heart. As you exhale, round your spine. Repeat.)

Look Inward How I feel in my body right now is . . . inhale through your nose . . . exhale through your nose.

When things are out of order, it makes me feel . . . inhale . . . exhale . . .

When I can't keep track or stay on top of things, it makes me feel . . . inhale . . . exhale . . .

Emit Hum three times.

Activate See it! Imagine a beautiful row of flowers, organized according to color and category so you can easily find them in a garden or nursery. Or a shelf of books or spices meticulously arranged in alphabetical order.

Nourish Feel it! What is the air like in the greenhouse? How does it smell, feel on your body? What is your experience walking down the row?

Surrender Say: "I allow calm. I allow focus. I allow removal. I allow sorting. I allow freedom."

Ease Say: "I calm. I am focused. I am releasing. I am removing. I am sorting. I am organized. I am free."

228

Cleansing Not Speaking Up

You are in a meeting or on a call and have a great idea, point to make, or correction to share but you can't quite bring yourself to express it. You continue to listen while inside you feel a tremendous amount of tension and discomfort. A part of you wants to speak up and say, "Hey we've got an issue here, people are upset, feeling rattled or unclear!" or "You're missing the point! What if we . . ." yet something inside of you tells you to be quiet, stay small, and not make waves. While this can be an okay strategy once in a while, when it becomes a chronic way of coping, it can repress feelings of resentment, anger, unworthiness, and shame. Maybe you were told that good girls keep quiet and stay sweet, or boys should suck it up, be men, and not act weak. While this might not consciously be the case for you, I find some of these old belief systems continue to seep through even though we know better. Nonetheless, trust in the processing of a CLEANSE now and be ready to contribute the next time your voice needs to be heard.

Clear Reactivity Sitting up tall, take your right thumb and close off your right nostril as you breathe in . . . and out . . . through your left nostril. Do this slowly and repeat three to five times in a row. Be sure to take it slow and inflate your abdomen on the inhale and deflate on the exhale. Release your hand, put it on your lap and observe your breathing for twenty seconds before you move to step two.

Look Inward How I feel in my body right now is . . . inhale through your nose . . . exhale through your nose.

When I can't speak up, it makes me feel . . . inhale . . . exhale . . .

Sensing the discomfort and tension in others makes me feel . . . inhale . . . exhale . . .

When I hold back my true self, it makes me feel . . . inhale . . . exhale . . .

Emit Hum three times.

Activate See it! Imagine an image of freeing, presence, and authenticity. Perhaps turning on a faucet to release a strong rush of water or a bird let out of a cage.

Nourish Feel it! Let your body soften and relax, letting go of any tension as you visualize your image.

Surrender Say: "I allow release. I allow surrender. I allow truth. I allow authenticity. I allow presence. I allow freedom."

Ease Say: "I am releasing. I am purifying. I am clear. I am truth. I am present. I am strong. I am free."

Cleansing Goals & Deadlines

Do you have certain goals, target dates, or benchmarks you need to reach? Is there are part of you that feels you are not reaching them? Maybe there is a sales number you need to hit, or you are in charge of increasing traffic on the company website or social media. Perhaps you have a book you are writing, or are preparing for a webinar, speaking engagement, or training and the people you work with are expecting quantifiable results. Maybe you feel like you don't have the resources to complete these projects or meet these goals. Maybe the ticking clock or looming deadline *demotivates* you instead of motivating you. If so, this CLEANSE is for you. Here is the thing, without a CLEANSE, your creative process, work rhythm, and best intentions can become bogged down by negative, fearful thinking. You may find yourself spending time worrying about the future, venting, and losing sleep because of work-related anxieties, none of which will help you with the task at hand.

Clear Reactivity Sit or stand up tall, close your eyes, and let gravity take over, pulling your navel toward your spine. Take a nice long exhale and squeeze the muscles of your pelvic floor. For women this will be a slight Kegel. Hold that squeeze for three to five seconds and then release as you exhale and allow your breath to flow. Repeat this sequence—squeeze . . . breathe—two or three more times. (Note: If you are pregnant, don't hold your breath at all.)

Look Inward How I feel in my body right now is . . . inhale through your nose . . . exhale through your nose.

Meeting deadlines makes me feel . . . inhale . . . exhale . . .

When I worry I won't be able to meet certain goals, it makes me feel . . . inhale . . . exhale . . .

Being rushed or pressured makes me feel . . . inhale . . . exhale . . .

Emit Hum three times.

Activate See it! Visualize an image of calm, stillness, and spaciousness. Perhaps you see a large body of water such as a calm ocean, a still lake, or a glacier.

Nourish Feel it! Imagine being near that body of water, breathing in the quiet and solitude. Notice how it refreshes your senses.

Surrender Say: "I allow refreshing. I allow energizing. I allow ease. I allow soothing. I allow focus. I allow calm."

Ease Say: "I am focused. I am refreshed. I am soothed. I am calm. I am confident. I am enough."

Cleansing Technology Issues

Can I please make an appointment?" I asked. "I am so sorry, but the computers have been down all morning. May I take your name and number and call you back?" replied the woman on the other end of the phone line. Sound familiar? In today's world we are so reliant on technology that without it we truly cannot function. As a matter of fact, as I write this book I am hoping and praying my computer doesn't break down on me—that would be a nightmare. *Oh dear! I have something CLEANSE.*

In this CLEANSE give yourself permission to release both the times technology fails as well as the fear of it failing or not working properly. Both things happen in the workplace and without a CLEANSE this could be an area where quite a bit of emotional energy gets trapped.

Clear Reactivity It's time to gargle. You can use plain water, water with a pinch of salt, or mouthwash. Take a sip and gargle for fifteen seconds or so. Spit and pause for a moment before moving to the next step.

Look Inward How I feel in my body right now is . . . inhale through your nose . . . exhale through your nose.

When technology becomes unreliable or inconsistent, it makes me feel . . . inhale . . . exhale . . .

The thought of having things break down makes me feel . . . inhale . . . exhale . . .

Emit Hum three times.

Activate See it! Visualize an image of assurance, calm, comfort, and efficiency. Imagine a windmill operating smoothly and effortlessly or a sailboat gliding across a lake.

Nourish Feel it! Imagine how it would feel to receive the energy of that windmill, move through the water on the sailboat. Notice your in breath and out breath.

Surrender Say: "I allow calm. I allow receiving. I allow comfort. I allow non-effort. I allow reassurance."

Ease Say: "I am comforted. I am calm. I am assured. I am effortless. I am receiving. I am free."

Cleansing When You Feel Like You Are Not Earning Enough Money

Are struggling to make ends meet? You may have a good job and earning money, yet it doesn't feel like enough when your paycheck doesn't cover all your expenses, credit card payments, or student loans. Know you are not alone. The cost of living continues to rise, many companies are cutting people's hours, and unemployment is at an all-time high. The cost of things like health insurance, phone plans, mortgage and rent, and food costs make it difficult for many families and individuals to stay above water.

While there certainly are no quick-fix answers, I do believe the CLEANSE can help with this. By cleansing we can release the reactivity we have around lack and the fear of not being or having enough, opening up a path toward solutions and perhaps even abundance.

Clear Reactivity Take a moment and reach your arms out to your sides holding them straight and parallel to the ground. You will look like the letter T. Gently move your arms forward in small circles and then backward as if your arms are two sides of a propeller. Do this for ten seconds forward and ten seconds backward. Do not count! Just breathe as you make your circles. Relax your arms and shoulders, straighten your spine, and observe your inhale . . . and exhale . . . and now move to step two.

Look Inward How I feel in my body right now is . . . inhale through your nose . . . exhale through your nose.

When I see my finances getting depleted, it makes me feel . . . inhale . . . exhale . . .

When money feels tight or scarce, it makes me feel . . . inhale . . . exhale . . .

Worrying about money makes me feel . . . inhale . . . exhale . . .

Emit Hum three times.

Activate See it! Visualize an image of energy, wealth, resources, calm, comfort, and the abundance in nature. Perhaps rich, dark soil inundated with minerals and nutrients, ready for planting.

Nourish Feel it! Imagine picking up the soil in your hands. Feel its texture, smell its earthy fragrance.

Surrender Say: "I allow resources. I allow plenty. I allow energy. I allow abundance. I allow comfort. I allow ease."

Ease Say: "I am prosperous. I am resourceful. I am enough. I am calm. I am comforted. I am ease."

Cleansing Criticism or Being Reprimanded

It happens to all of us! Perhaps your manager spoke to you about following the wrong protocol, miscalculating a payment, being late, or missing a deadline. You might have found yourself reacting by becoming defensive. This is likely because even though you know we all make mistakes, there is a part of you that carries some unprocessed emotions of guilt and shame. Sometimes this can happen if you grew up in an environment where you always felt like you should have been doing better or more than you did, were compared to others, or were scolded for even the smallest infraction. Left unprocessed these memories support reactive behaviors such as defensiveness, needing to explain yourself, or even fudging the truth.

Clear Reactivity Sit up tall in a chair with both feet flat on the floor, hip-width apart. Reach your right hand to the back of the chair (you might have to scoot forward a bit) and turn to the right as you give your spine a gentle twist right. Release and return to center. Repeat on the other side, reaching with your left hand as you twist to the left. Hold each side for three counts before returning to center.

Look Inward How I feel in my body right now is . . . inhale through your nose . . . exhale through your nose.

The thought of being called out or spoken to makes me feel . . . inhale . . . exhale . . .

When I feel I have been bad, wrong, or am in trouble, it makes me feel . . . inhale . . . exhale . . .

Emit Hum three times.

Activate See it! Visualize an image of safety, trust, love, and kindness. Maybe a quiet bench in a park where you can peacefully enjoy the view.

Nourish Feel it! Imagine being in a place where you could let your guard down and allow the energy in your body to be free. Exhale.

Surrender Say: "I allow calm. I allow safety. I allow imperfection. I allow trust. I allow love. I allow compassion. I allow freedom."

Ease Say: "I am love. I am safe. I am trusting. I am compassionate. I am unique. I am worthy. I am calm. I am free."

Cleansing
Burnout

Have you ever used up all your vacation time, family leave, and sick days? Or maybe the schedule where you work is so tight you can't take the time you are technically owed. Maybe you are in the middle of major life transition—you just had a baby and or a loved one is sick. Perhaps you have an opportunity to take a vacation, but the team's schedule won't allow it. Maybe people have been laid off so you have to cover for them. It might be as simple as never getting a break for lunch. Without a CLEANSE, these situations can produce feelings of deprivation, resentment, and frustration. Right now you may feel like there is nothing you can do, you have no choice in the matter, and it is a no-win situation. Before you go down that rabbit hole, remember you can always use this as an opportunity to defuse reactivity and heal the feelings the circumstances are stirring up. What do you have to lose?

Clear Reactivity Sit on the floor and stretch your legs out a bit. If sitting on the floor is not possible then stand and lean on the wall if you need to. Either way, make sure your legs are stretched. If you

239

are on the floor, place your legs in a butterfly position with the soles of your feet together and knees wide as you lean forward into the stretch. Or you can press against the wall and stretch by hugging one knee in and then the other, or grabbing one foot in a quad stretch. The point is to activate those long muscles in your legs. Do what intuitively feels right for you and breathe into the stretch for at least one minute.

Look Inward How I feel in my body right now is . . . inhale through your nose . . . exhale through your nose.

Balancing work with my personal needs makes me feel . . . inhale and exhale.

When I miss fun activities with my family and friends, it makes me feel . . . inhale . . . exhale . . .

When I feel stuck or I have no choice in the matter, it makes me feel . . . inhale . . . exhale . . .

Emit Hum three times.

Activate See it! Visualize an image free of restraint, full of passion and zeal. Perhaps leaves or petals blowing in a wild wind, someone singing, or birds swooping in the sky.

Nourish Feel it! Imagine how would it feel to spread your wings, and let yourself soar, free from all perceived restrictions.

Surrender Say: "I allow freedom. I allow limitlessness. I allow presence. I allow connection. I allow release."

Ease Say: "I am releasing. I am open. I am compassionate. I am present. I am choosing. I am grounded. I am free."

Part V

HEALTH & WELL-BEING

Processed emotions become spiritual medicine and nourish not just our minds and bodies, but our spirits as well.

Sherianna, I am worried about my weight," stated a client. "I try not to let it bother me, but I know deep down inside it does. I am at the point where I just want to give up." As we dug into a CLEANSE, my client began to uncover the anger and frustration that was weighing her down. At times she would express how she was feeling, yet most of the time she found herself holding back, resisting not just her true feelings but also the hurt she had been carrying. What ultimately happened with her? Through the process of cleansing, she was able recognize and heal some of the criticism she received from her mother growing up. I knew things were changing for her when she started to focus less on her weight and more on activities like swimming, yoga, and nature walks. Her body was changing for the better. She was getting stronger, leaner, and her relationship with her mother improved. She no longer reviewed memories of hurt and instead focused on her better qualities while giving herself the gift of forgiveness.

Health and wellness are so much more than what you eat, how much you exercise, or even the way you cope with stress. They are also interconnected with the way you process those past hurts, renew your perspective, and give yourself the opportunity to strengthen your spiritual connection. When it comes to good health there are many paths of treatment and varieties of healthcare providers to consult. You can support any sort of physical treatment by doing things such as taking slow deep breaths a few times a day, spending time in nature, eating nutritious foods, taking supplements, seeking out clean air and water, and getting exercise—all of which may boost your immune system and overall levels of functioning. Of course, a CLEANSE can't directly heal illness, but it can nurture a mental and spiritual foundation upon which restoration and recovery can more freely and even rapidly occur—it can create the environment for optimal healing. That's because there is a deeper component that can impact our physical healing and psychological well-being—unprocessed emotions, unhealed wounds, and fears within us. So many of us continue to struggle, despite our best efforts and intentions. If we don't detox and digest our emotions, each one can leave an energetic blueprint or unconscious memory of a time you felt you needed to guard or protect yourself from harm. As you CLEANSE, these internal walls will gradually dissolve, leaving you with more space and time to take care of yourself. Not only to help prevent disease, facilitate healing, or even improve your health, but because you will find when you connect to the CLEANSE space inside of you, you will discover parts of yourself you never really allowed yourself to fully own. If you are not sure what those parts are, trust that the CLEANSE process will reveal them to you. While you might be accustomed to turning to the medical community for answers when things are not right, the CLEANSE encourages you to turn inward, discover your own healing abilities in conjunction with your medical providers. Staying updated with your medical providers allows you to receive feedback and reinforcement along the way.

Cleansing a Poor Night's Sleep

There is nothing worse than a rough night's sleep. Tossing and turning and wakefulness can occur for a number of reasons—being too hot or cold, a noisy environment, overuse of technology, intrusive anxious thoughts, light pollution, dehydration, caffeine, or hunger. But we all need sleep! According to the National Institute of Neurological Disorders and Stroke, "sleep removes toxins in your brain that build up while you are awake. Furthermore, research shows that a chronic lack of sleep, or getting poor quality sleep, increases the risk of disorders including high blood pressure, cardiovascular disease, diabetes, depression, and obesity."[5]

To support yourself, consider installing blackout shades, creating a wind-down routine like drinking herbal tea or taking a warm shower before bed, perhaps taking magnesium and calcium supplements, or dumping all your worries or things to do in a journal before bed. As you might have guessed, a CLEANSE before sleeping can help too.

Clear Reactivity About thirty minutes before you go to bed, lie on your back, head on a pillow, and (if you are able) place your legs on the wall. You can put a yoga mat, pillows, or blanket underneath your legs for comfort. Breathe into your lower abdomen area as you move through this CLEANSE.

Look Inward How I feel in my body right now is . . . inhale through your nose . . . exhale through your nose.

Winding down from this day makes me feel . . . inhale . . . exhale . . .

Loosening my body makes me feel . . . inhale . . . exhale . . .

Tuning in to my inner self now makes me feel . . . inhale . . . exhale . . .

Emit Hum three times.

Activate See it! Visualize a release, calm, letting go, surrender, and peace that is as effortless as the way you might release a handful of sand back onto the beach.

Nourish Feel it! Imagine what it would be like to squeeze the sand in your hand and then let it go.

Surrender Say: "I allow release. I allow surrender. I allow freedom. I allow digestion. I allow feeling."

Ease Say: "I am feeling. I am receiving. I am surrender. I am at peace. I am free."

Cleansing When You Feel a Little Off

There are times when you might not feel well. Perhaps you have a headache, an aching back, or you mentally just aren't yourself. Maybe you are a bit down in the dumps, grumpy, negative, or are feeling more weary than usual. While it is normal to have off days, those times when your body might need a little extra tender loving care, when a few days stretches into a week or a month of something not feeling quite right, you might want to check in with your doctor. The purpose of this CLEANSE is to help you release whatever may be showing up for you psychologically. Experiences, situations, emotions that may be causing you strain and leaving you mentally and physically depleted.

Clear Reactivity Press the pads of both of your middle fingers together, while leaving the other fingers loose. Hold them near your navel as you inhale and exhale gently through your nose for approximately thirty seconds.

Look Inward How I feel in my body right now is . . . inhale through your nose . . . exhale through your nose.

Tuning in to my body right now makes me feel . . . inhale . . . exhale . . .

Tuning in to my brain right now makes me feel . . . inhale . . . exhale . . .

Tuning in to my spirit right now makes me feel . . . inhale . . . exhale . . .

Emit Hum three times.

Activate See it! Visualize health, wellness, vitality, energy, happiness, and freedom. Maybe what it's like to peel and open up an orange—that sudden burst of fragrance and sweetness.

Nourish Feel it! Imagine what it would feel like to have a natural, vibrant glowing energy inside and out.

Surrender Say: "I allow health. I allow wellness. I allow vitality. I allow energy. I allow happiness. I allow freedom."

Ease Say: "I am healthy. I am well. I am vital. I am energetic. I am hopeful. I am free."

Cleansing Feeling Undeserving

One of the subconscious beliefs that can interfere with the healing process is the belief that you don't deserve it. However, it can be difficult to know if you are carrying this belief, so here is one way to find out. Maybe you said something hurtful to or about someone. Now let's imagine that person finds out: how would that make you feel? Bad? Guilty? Embarrassed? While these emotions are normal and healthy, they can be very uncomfortable. As a result, you may have developed a belief (*I don't deserve better*) as a way to cope with the pain you believe you have caused.

I have seen this so often in my Emotional Detox practice—people unconsciously sabotage themselves because somewhere along the line they developed the belief that they were not good enough, were undeserving or unworthy. Here is something I think you ought to know: If this were really true, you would not be drawn to this book. As you can see by now, each time you CLEANSE, you are connecting to the aspect of you that is worthy, powerful, capable, and strong. You would not go through the process if you did not believe in the possibility.

Clear Reactivity Sit up tall, chin parallel to the earth, with both feet touching the ground hip-width apart. With your palm facing out, take your right arm and wrap it around your lower back until you feel a stretch in your right rotator-cuff muscle. If for some reason this bothers your shoulder, hold your arm out straight to the side at a height a little below your shoulder and stretch it that way. Place your arm back by your side and repeat with the left arm as you stretch your left shoulder. Place both hands on your lap in front, pause, take one deep breath . . . inhale . . . exhale . . . and proceed.

Look Inward How I feel in my body right now is . . . inhale through your nose . . . exhale through your nose.

When I do not feel worthy, it makes me feel . . . inhale . . . exhale . . .

Carrying this in my body now makes me feel . . . inhale . . . exhale . . .

Connecting to higher aspects of myself now makes me feel . . . inhale . . . exhale . . .

Emit Hum three times.

Activate See it! Visualize a blessing, goodness, kindness, compassion, and love. Perhaps an image of someone you love serving you a healthy and delicious meal.

Nourish Feel it! Imagine what it would feel like to receive and value being offered this wonderful food.

Surrender Say: "I allow value. I allow blessings. I allow receiving. I allow worth. I allow deserving. I allow approval."

Ease Say: "I am approval. I am honored. I am blessings. I am worthy. I am free."

Cleansing
Emotional Eating

Emotional eating occurs when someone uses food as a way to filter, distract from, or soothe negative and uncomfortable emotions, especially stress. Since stress can impact the cortisol (stress hormone) levels in the body and induce hunger, this can disrupt your mind-body signals, making it difficult to know the difference between stress, true hunger, and boredom. Emotional eating can also happen when you need a mental boost or want to give yourself a little reward. The challenge is these "indulgences" can quickly turn into habits. To support yourself, begin to pay attention to the way you eat. Consider keeping a little journal and writing down the times you eat (when you can't sleep in the night or when you get groggy after lunch) and what is going on in your life (a looming deadline or a child leaving home for the first time). Also notice if food has become a method of a distraction, a way to avoid dealing with stress or handling tasks and responsibilities. This is a good one to do before you reach for that snack.

Clear Reactivity Take a moment and look around for something to hold in your hand. Ideally, something from the earth—a stone, crystal, or leaf. Breathe in and out through your nose as you feel the weight of this object in your hands. Allow the presence of the object to anchor your breath to the now for thirty to sixty seconds.

Look Inward How I feel in my body right now is . . . inhale through your nose . . . exhale through your nose.

When I turn to food, it makes me feel . . . inhale . . . exhale . . .

When I become bored or restless food makes me feel . . . inhale . . . exhale . . .

Tuning in to my body right now makes me feel . . . inhale . . . exhale . . .

Emit Hum three times.

Activate See it! Visualize energy, fullness, life, happiness, safety, peace, and freedom. Where would you go in nature or in your home to feel a sense of wholeness? Think of what you love or are passionate about. For me it is a bookstore. Someone who loves music might discover this feeling at a musical festival.

Nourish Feel it! Imagine everything you need is with you now— love, comfort, healing, safety, worthiness, and purpose. It is all in this place and moment. Breathe into the sensation.

Surrender Say: "I allow freedom. I allow wholeness. I allow fullness. I allow breath. I allow life. I allow transformation."

Ease Say: "I am free. I am alive. I am full. I am breath. I am transformation."

Cleansing
External Pressure

When it comes to getting healthy you may be experiencing quite a bit of pressure. Maybe your doctor is getting on your case about decreasing your cholesterol levels and encouraging you to eat better and exercise more. Maybe your family is expressing concerns about your health. Perhaps you took some time to research a plan, came up with alternatives to traditional medicine, and your healthcare provider dismissed your approach. Or maybe you have received divergent medical options and don't know which one to choose—and let's face it, when it comes to the healthcare industry there is no shortage of opinions. After considering your options you must make decision and plan a course of action that feels right for you. So to support you in your journey toward caring for yourself take a moment now and CLEANSE.

Clear Reactivity Interlace your fingers, turn your palms outward, and bring your arms away from your body and over your head. It will feel like a nice big stretch. Inhale and exhale, and now release your arms back by your sides. Repeat this sequence two or three more times.

Look Inward How I feel in my body right now is . . . inhale through your nose . . . exhale through your nose.

When I feel like I am doing something wrong or I could make a mistake, it makes me feel . . . inhale . . . exhale . . .

Having this pressure on me makes me feel . . . inhale . . . exhale . . .

Emit Hum three times.

Activate See it! Visualize an image of release, surrender, relaxation, and calm. Perhaps the image of a butterfly flitting among lovely flowers.

Nourish Feel it! How does it feel to watch this butterfly move with ease and calm?

Surrender Say: "I allow release. I allow surrender. I allow freedom. I allow trust."

Ease Say: "I am releasing. I am clear. I am calm. I am trusting. I am okay. I am safe. I am free."

Cleansing Social Media

Be honest with me—how much time do you spend each day on social media? It turns out, each time you read a "like" or a comment it triggers the reward system in your brain. You literally get a shot of dopamine—the hormone associated with pleasure and reward—every single time. The challenge is, it quickly fades . . . that is until you check it again. Also, since we can turn to social media for this burst of pleasure we don't spend time with the people around us or in solitude or contemplation.

You can thank technology for this. It's no accident that developers have created things like that continuous scroll option, the alert reminders, or ads that pop up in relation to your searches to keep you on your social media even longer, getting you ever more addicted. With anxiety and rates of depression at an all-time high it is no secret social media is having a strong negative impact on our mental health, hence the reason for this CLEANSE.

Clear Reactivity Take a moment and with the pointer and middle finger or your right hand tap the edge of your left between the base of your pinkie and wrist at the "karate chop" point. Do this for about thirty seconds. Then, with your left hand, again using your pointer and middle finger, tap the same point on your right. Notice how your breath shifts. Continue tapping as you move through the remainder of the CLEANSE.

Look Inward How I feel in my body right now is . . . inhale through your nose . . . exhale through your nose.

When someone likes or comments on my posts, it makes me feel . . . inhale . . . exhale . . .

When the likes are few or nobody comments, it makes me feel . . . inhale . . . exhale . . .

Checking social media makes me feel . . . inhale . . . exhale . . .

Not checking social media makes me feel . . . inhale . . . exhale . . .

Emit Hum three times.

Activate See it! Visualize an image of something readily genuine, evident, and tangible. For example, the difference between watching a live performance and seeing it on television.

Nourish Feel it! Pay attention to the difference in your body. The sounds, the vibe, the shared experience with the people around you.

Surrender Say: "I allow alive. I allow being seen. I allow being heard. I allow sounds. I allow presence. I allow stimulation."

Ease Say: "I am stimulation. I am seen. I am heard. I am present. I am alive. I am well. I am free."

Cleansing Discomfort with Your Age

We're all getting older, there's no way to stop it! While some people might embrace the idea of getting up in years, others may have a harder time. I remember when my husband was looking for a new job and felt his age was working against him. Each time he was choosing a picture of himself to post on LinkedIn he would ask, "Which one makes me look younger?" Age comes up quite a bit with my clients. Some feel a sense of urgency to hurry up and get married and have children, while others see age as a barrier to their fitness levels, health, relationships, freedom, and more. Perhaps you tend to speak negatively about your age, saying things like "You better enjoy that now, because you won't when you're my age." Or maybe you are experiencing natural changes in your body, like not being able to exercise as much and needing more rest. Maybe you feel like you should have accomplished more by now. Without awareness, you can repress emotions related to incompetency, inferiority, low self-esteem, or even the idea of being a burden. Holding on to such emotions certainly won't make you feel any younger, but a CLEANSE will.

Clear Reactivity Take a moment to wrap your arms around yourself. Yes, you heard me, give yourself a big hug. Notice how your body instantly wants to take a breath as you hold this squeeze. Then, unwrap your arms, placing the opposite arm on top and as you hug yourself again. Pause. Breathe in . . . and out.

Look Inward How I feel in my body right now is . . . inhale through your nose . . . exhale through your nose.

Being this age makes me feel . . . inhale . . . exhale . . .

When I am around people who are younger or older than I am, it makes me feel . . . inhale . . . exhale . . .

When I no longer see myself as a number, it makes me feel . . . inhale . . . exhale . . .

Emit Hum three times.

Activate See it! Visualize an image of youth, freshness, activity, and blossoming. Perhaps images of springtime, like baby birds, seedlings emerging from the ground, and trees in bloom.

Nourish Feel it! Imagine the sensation of the spring air, hearing the birds chirp, the fragrance of the flowers.

Surrender Say: "I allow confidence. I allow freshness. I allow vitality. I allow wholeness. I allow happiness."

Ease Say: "I am whole. I am grateful. I am calm. I am healthy. I am happy. I am free."

257

Cleansing Anxiety

Before beginning this CLEANSE, I want you to know I wrote an entire book on this topic—*Emotional Detox for Anxiety*. So if you are someone who wakes up and/or goes to bed obsessing and worrying, consider reading that book. But for now, the main thing you ought to know about anxiety is you do not need a reason for having it. Anxiety means your brain and body have gotten caught up in a reactive loop. With that said, any of the CLEANSEs in this book will help you break up those patterns. You see, anxiety and emotional flow cannot coexist. In another words, anxiety feeds off thoughts not feelings, and from the Emotional Detox perspective, fearful thoughts are not feelings, they are reactions.

Clear Reactivity Tone your vagus nerve by taking your right thumb and blocking off your right nostril so you are fully breathing through the left nostril. Be sure to sit up tall when you breathe and keep your legs uncrossed with both feet parallel, hip-width apart. Inhale through the left nostril . . . one . . . two . . . three . . . and exhale through the left nostril . . . four . . . three . . . two . . . one. Your navel will contract, moving toward the spine on the exhale.

Look Inward How I feel in my body right now is . . . inhale through your nose . . . exhale through your nose.

When I acknowledge that I have anxiety, it makes me feel . . . inhale . . . exhale . . .

When I try to get better, it makes me feel . . . inhale . . . exhale . . .

Living life in this way makes me feel . . . inhale . . . exhale . . .

Emit Hum three times.

Activate See it! Visualize peace, calm, steadiness, security, and gratitude. Maybe it's somewhere you can sense and feel pure peace on your skin, maybe a snowy mountain, a moving stream, or a sunset.

Nourish Feel it! What is it like to be in a serene and beautiful setting? What do you hear? What do you see?

Surrender Say: "I allow movement. I allow release. I allow grounding. I allow hope. I allow relinquishing."

Ease Say: "I am relinquishing. I am moving. I am transforming. I am grounded. I am love. I am free."

Cleansing
Addictive
Behavior

According to the American Psychiatric Association, "Addiction is a brain disease that is manifested by compulsive substance use despite harmful consequences. People with addiction have an intense focus on the substance to the point where it takes over their life."[6] When it comes to incorporating the Emotional Detox perspective into supporting yourself or others through the recovery and healing process, here is the way I see it: addiction is an extreme form of control. It is an intense (in some cases, extreme) pattern of pushing emotional energy away and suppressing it, and it shows up in many forms. You can be addicted to food, sex, pornography, work, alcohol, or drugs. You can also be addicted to things like self-criticism, avoidance, anger, or praise. The challenge is that the more you push, the less energy or awareness you have, and this inevitably makes you feel powerless or out of control. I am not saying addiction isn't a disease in the brain, however, I do believe it is possible to rewire and heal your brain, and a CLEANSE will help.

Clear Reactivity Splashing your face daily with freezing water can help you tone your vagus nerve. Making this chilly water splash a part of your regular routine will strengthen your connection to step one of this and any CLEANSE.

Look Inward How I feel in my body right now is . . . inhale through your nose . . . exhale through your nose.

Having these thoughts, urges, and desires makes me feel . . . inhale . . . exhale . . .

When I push away my emotions, it makes me feel . . . inhale . . . exhale . . . nice and slow.

Tuning in to myself now makes me feel . . . inhale . . . exhale . . .

Emit Hum three times and pause to appreciate how it soothes you.

Activate See it! Visualize an image of soothing, comfort, pure love, healing, and surrender. The view from an overlook on a mountaintop or the sensation of sinking into a bubble bath.

Nourish Feel it! Bring yourself to a place in your mind where you can feel comfort and allow surrender. Perhaps it's the immersion in the warm bathwater or the quiet on that mountaintop. It's up to you to choose.

Surrender Say: "I allow calm. I allow disinterest. I allow indifference. I allow peace. I allow healing."

Ease Say: "I am healing. I am at peace. I am impartial. I am healing. I am love. I am free."

Cleansing Pain

Do you live with chronic pain? Perhaps you have discomfort in your knees, hips, or lower back when you walk. Or maybe the pain you live with is in your heart—a deep ache and longing for some relief. You may find the pain you experience comes and goes. One day you feel good and then the next day you may be really struggling. This no doubt can have an impact on your mental health. Sure, the good days may give you a boost, put an extra skip in your step and a smile on your face, but the bad days can weigh on you, causing you to feel overwhelmed, insecure, and in some cases weary and depressed. As a result you may start turning down invitations to connect with people—like parties or other gatherings—and isolating yourself, or you may wake up dreading getting out of bed. This CLEANSE gives you an opportunity to release some of those suppressed emotions around the pain you are carrying.

Clear Reactivity Make a fist and gently tap your chest area for about thirty seconds. Allow this thumping action to break up any congested energy around your heart center.

Look Inward How I feel in my body right now is . . . inhale through your nose . . . exhale through your nose.

When I wake up in the morning I feel . . . inhale . . . exhale . . .

Managing pain makes me feel . . . inhale . . . exhale . . .

When it gets out of control I feel . . . inhale . . . exhale . . .

Emit Hum three to five times. As you do, remember to consider humming whenever early signs of pain arise.

Activate See it! Visualize an image of relief. What would it look like? A kite flying in the air or a volcano erupting? Take a moment to notice.

Nourish Feel it! Imagine how the kite string would tug and release in your hands.

Surrender Say: "I allow light. I allow relief. I allow freedom. I allow movement. I allow release."

Ease Say: "I am light. I am relief. I am capable. I am movement. I am energy. I am free."

Cleansing Transitions

Transitions can have a significant impact on your health. This is because you have to adjust to a new way of living your life, a new course of action, a new series of patterns both physically and mentally. For some of us this might be adapting to online classes after years of attending in-person school. Perhaps you are adjusting to having your child in daycare or adapting to a new schedule at work. Maybe it's a major life transition such as divorce, death of a loved one, or losing a job. Sometimes transitions can be about adjusting to a new season, changing from the freedom of fall to the limitations and darkness of winter. Or perhaps you are trying to find a way to incorporate more exercise into your life, drink a little less coffee, or eat more wholesome foods. Transitions big and small take time and therefore require patience. A CLEANSE can be a way of fostering the energy of patience.

Clear Reactivity Rub your hands together vigorously for about thirty seconds. Separate them and place your dominant hand on your forehead and the other hand on your lower abdomen. Breathe in . . . and out . . . through your nose for thirty seconds. As you do this, inflate your abdomen on the inhale as you connect your brain and gut.

Look Inward How I feel in my body right now is . . . inhale through your nose . . . exhale through your nose.

Adjusting to new situations, people, and schedules makes me feel . . . inhale . . . exhale . . .

When things seem off-balance or unfamiliar, I feel . . . inhale . . . exhale . . .

Emit Hum three times.

Activate See it! Imagine an image of a memory of comfort. Perhaps a cozy blanket or soft pillow you loved as a child.

Nourish Feel it! What would it feel like to have that comforting object with you right now? Notice how it soothes and connects you to the present.

Surrender Say: "I allow comfort. I allow familiarity. I allow calm. I allow change. I allow patience. I allow reassurance."

Ease Say: "I am reassured. I am comforted. I am ease. I am patient. I am change. I am free."

Cleansing Expectations

Do you expect a lot from yourself or the people in our life? In other words, do you get easily disappointed, have unattainable standards, or a challenging time celebrating what you achieve? Maybe you compare yourself to others or find yourself noticing what is wrong more often than what is right. When it comes to your health and well-being, it is not expectations that are the problem but rather becoming overly attached to them. You may do this by perseverating on ideas, conversations, or problem-solving. Without realizing it, this can cause you great distress, irritability, and restlessness. Ask yourself: Do I expect too much from myself, and if so, how might this impact what I expect in others? In other words, if I expect myself to take on the weight of the world, does that in turn cause me to expect others to do the same? When you don't live up to what you expect how might that impact the emotional health of your relationships? As you move through this CLEANSE, I encourage you to be kind and gentle on yourself.

Clear Reactivity Tilt your head left to right, holding for one second on each side. Repeat this movement until your breath starts to naturally kick in. Be gentle with your neck and allow your shoulders to soften before moving your head and neck in the opposite direction.

Look Inward How I feel in my body right now is . . . inhale through your nose . . . exhale through your nose.

Experiencing this pressure right now makes me feel . . . inhale . . . exhale . . .

And when these expectations influence my emotional well-being (e.g., balance, focus, flow), it makes me feel . . . inhale . . . exhale . . .

Being kind, gentle, and loving with myself makes me feel . . . inhale . . . exhale . . .

Emit Hum three times.

Activate See it! Visualize an image of detachment. Perhaps a vine unwrapping from a tree, releasing its grip on the trunk.

Nourish Feel it! How would it feel to tug on that vine and give the tree some space to breathe?

Surrender Say: "I allow movement. I allow freedom. I allow release. I allow non-effort. I allow surrender."

Ease Say: "I am movement. I am free. I am released. I am surrendering. I am gentle. I am ease."

Cleansing Fear

The feeling of fear can either stop you in your tracks (freeze), cause you to get out of the situation in any way possible (flight), or argue and assert control over something (fight). Fear can arise from something you imagine like a family member getting into an accident, or a real threat such as someone suddenly screaming at you. You know you are in a state of fear when your heart rate speeds up or you abruptly become speechless. When it comes time to CLEANSE pent-up fearful emotions, especially around your health, think of fear as the bridge between uncertainty and peace. You see, the discomfort you may or may not feel when your body is attempting to process an emotion is a sign you are right at the edge of completing your work on something old (perhaps an old buried emotion) so you can receive something new, like the experience of feeling powerful, bold, brave, faithful, and ultimately fearless.

Clear Reactivity Rub and squeeze the back of your neck with your hand for a minute. As you give yourself this little massage, pause and breathe . . . inhale . . . and exhale . . . before you move to step two.

Look Inward How I feel in my body right now is . . . inhale through your nose . . . exhale through your nose.

Tuning in to my breath right now makes me feel . . . inhale . . . exhale . . .

When I bring my attention to my feet and legs, it makes me feel . . . inhale . . . exhale . . .

Releasing this pent-up energy now makes me feel . . . inhale . . . exhale . . .

Emit Hum three times.

Activate See it! Visualize an image of calm, presence, curiosity, and wonder. Perhaps it's the taste of a new yummy food or a kitten discovering a toy for the first time.

Nourish Feel it! Imagine how you feel when you experience curiosity.

Surrender Say: "I allow curious. I allow calm. I allow wonder. I allow presence. I allow trust."

Ease Say: "I am calm. I am trusting. I am wondering. I am present. I am free."

Cleansing Dread

Think about a time you felt apprehensive, angst, or worry about doing something. Perhaps it was attending a social event or a parent-teacher conference. Maybe it was a trip to the doctor or the results of a test. At first it sounded like a promising idea—you'd get to meet new people or get some answers—but as the date approached you found yourself uneasy about it. Perhaps you are awaiting a court date to discuss child custody. Or maybe it's something positive like a new job or a wedding that still holds just enough uncertainty to evoke dread. Without a CLEANSE, situations such as these can cause tremendous amounts of stress. While having some stress can be a good thing as it can give you the courage to show up for that appointment, when it becomes chronic and overwhelming it can have a negative impact on your mental and physical health. So let's CLEANSE dread.

Clear Reactivity While sitting up tall, both feet flat on the floor, hip-width apart, cross your arms in front of your body with each hand holding the opposite elbow. Keeping your arms folded in this way, make a small spinal twist to the right (you won't get too far) and hold for three seconds. Return to center and inhale . . . then on the exhale twist to the other side. Move back to center and inhale . . . exhale . . . before going to step two.

Look Inward How I feel in my body right now is . . . inhale through your nose . . . exhale through your nose.

When I have to do something I do not want to do, it makes me feel . . . inhale . . . exhale . . .

Being in these situations makes me feel . . . inhale . . . exhale . . .

Emit Hum three times.

Activate See it! Visualize an image of praise, approval, and celebration. Perhaps sparkling festive fireworks illuminating a summer sky!

Nourish Feel it! What would it feel like to watch fireworks, see their color, or hear the vibrations as they crackle?

Surrender Say: "I allow praise. I allow victory. I allow happiness. I allow love. I allow calm."

Ease Say: "I am whole. I am victorious. I am calm. I am happy. I am love. I am free."

Cleansing Anger and Control

Are you feeling frustrated with your situation? When it comes to your health, are you sick and tired of people telling you what to do? Or maybe just sick and tired of being sick and tired? Or maybe you are feeling like the future of your health is being held in someone else's hands and that makes you feel powerless—like you have very little say in the matter. You want to trust the system, believe that those who are supporting you (or a loved one) have your best interests at heart, yet there is a part of you that has had enough. No matter what you do, your situation does not seem to change much. Here is the thing, when it comes to your mental and physical well-being it is important that you feel safe, heard, and validated. It is important you have agency. While I am certainly not telling you what to do, what I do know is before you do, say, or change anything it is important to CLEANSE and take time to feel what is coming up in you to be released.

Clear Reactivity Take a moment now and yawn. Yes, yawn. Go ahead, open your mouth wide and let a big old "ahh" emerge. If you said to yourself, "But that will make me tired and I do not want to be tired," it's exactly that negating, controlling voice you want this CLEANSE to deactivate.

Look Inward How I feel in my body right now is . . . inhale through your nose . . . exhale through your nose.

When I do not know what the outcome will be I . . . inhale . . . exhale . . .

When I do not have a say, it makes me feel . . . inhale . . . exhale . . .

And when I do not feel seen, heard, or validated, it makes me feel . . . inhale . . . exhale . . .

Emit Hum three times.

Activate See it! Visualize an image of carefree trust, pleasant serenity. Maybe being outside on a perfect spring day.

Nourish Feel it! Imagine what it would feel like to be in mild temperatures or to sit on a porch swing with a cool glass of water. Let all your fears and worries go.

Surrender Say: "I allow carefree. I allow attentive. I allow mild. I allow calm. I allow centered."

Ease Say: "I am carefree. I am attentive. I am calm. I am trusting. I am surrendering. I am free."

Cleansing Disappointment

So you received some disappointing news, or maybe you are bummed out by your lack of progress at work, school, in a relationship, or with a health issue. You are just not seeing the changes you had expected. Maybe you gained rather than lost a pound. (*Ugh . . . that is one of the reasons I do not own a scale.*) Or perhaps you gave up cheese, but your cholesterol levels stayed the same. Or maybe your grades weren't what you hoped they would be, you didn't get asked on a second date, or you were looked over for a promotion.

Without a CLEANSE, the emotion of disappointment can create a weight in your heart, uncertain thoughts, and a sense of doubt. Left unresolved these emotions get only heavier, leaving you with a sense of sadness. You may be tempted to manage your feelings of disappointment by reviewing all the shoulds, whys, and should-nots in your mind: *I should have said this. If I'd only done that.* While there might be a part of you that wishes you could go back in time, redo the event, try something different, I suggest you let go of all that and allow the

CLEANSE to create space around it. You see, underneath all that disappointment may be aspects of yourself looking to release patterns of self-judgment and shame.

Clear Reactivity Sit up tall, chin parallel to the earth. Take the two peace-sign fingers of your dominant hand and press about an inch above your navel. Shift the pressure slightly to the right, and then slightly to the left as you stimulate your three acupressure points. Keep the pressure light and don't forget to breathe.

Look Inward How I feel in my body right now is . . . inhale through your nose . . . exhale through your nose.

Carrying this heaviness in my heart makes me feel . . . inhale . . . exhale . . .

When I try to move on and forget, it makes me feel . . . inhale . . . exhale . . .

Emit Hum three times.

Activate See it! Visualize love, tenderness, and compassion. Perhaps something in nature like a calm lake, a single flower in a vase, or a monarch butterfly.

Nourish Feel it! Imagine gazing at that gentle lake, soft beautiful flower, or delicate butterfly.

Surrender Say: "I allow love. I allow compassion. I allow forgiveness. I allow freedom."

Ease Say: "I am love. I am compassion. I am energy. I am enough. I am free."

Cleansing Stigma

This CLEANSE is for those of you who have felt discriminated against, discredited, or shamed for being disabled or having a mental health diagnosis. While attention in the media and concentrated efforts like mental health awareness month have helped ease the stigma a bit, it is important for each and every one of us to contribute to the cause by taking a moment to individually CLEANSE. Here is the thing about a CLEANSE—while you may have not been the cause of your stigmatization, you can be part of the solution. The reality is, these stigmas have affected us all, maybe not directly, but indirectly. You see, what I love about the CLEANSE is it brings me to a place where we are all one. There is no this or that, good or bad, ability or disability, us or other in the CLEANSE realm. I believe the more time we spend in the energy of this space the closer we will get to experiencing more compassion and unity. So let's do our part now and begin.

Clear Reactivity Sit or stand up very tall. Take a very deep breathe in through your nose as you inflate your lower abdomen. Exhale through your nose and deflate your abdomen. Keeping your attention on your lower abdomen slowly allow it to fill up with oxygen for a count of one . . . two . . . three . . . and then on the exhale pull your navel inward toward your spine for a count of one . . . two . . . three . . . four. Pause before you proceed to step two.

~~~~~

Look Inward How I feel in my body right now is . . . inhale through your nose . . . exhale through your nose.

~~~~~

Sensing the energy of shame makes me feel . . . inhale . . . exhale . . .

~~~~~

When the energy of judgment arises in me, it makes me feel . . . inhale . . . exhale . . .

~~~~~

Emit Hum three times.

~~~~~

Activate See it! Visualize in your mind's eye an image of worthiness, significance, honor, and respect. Perhaps an image of the mountains, rivers, or even the majesty of the Grand Canyon!

~~~~~

Nourish Feel it! Imagine what it would feel like to stand in front of a regal mountain or look across the expanse of the Grand Canyon. Allow this powerful energy to move through you now.

~~~~~

Surrender Say: "I allow worthy. I allow significance. I allow honor. I allow grace."

~~~~~

Ease Say: "I am honor. I am respect. I am significant. I am grace."

Cleansing Your Immune System

Sometimes I wonder which is worse, getting sick or having a fear of getting sick. Think of your cells as little communicators constantly responding to your thoughts and bodily reactions. While things like taking vitamin C or zinc supplements, dedicating time to rest, washing your hands, drinking plenty of fluids, and keeping your home clean can enhance or protect your immune system, I believe a large part of remaining healthy is a result of taking time to process your emotions. Apparently I am not alone, as Hilary Jacobs Hendel wrote in *Time* magazine, "When people are given education on emotions and skills for how to work with them, they can begin to feel better. The role that emotions play in creating both physical suffering and healing is becoming a more popular focus in psychotherapy."[7] Making CLEANSE a part of your self-care routine will help.

Clear Reactivity Pour yourself a glass of ice-cold water and take some small sips as you inhale . . . exhale . . . in between each sip. Repeat this a few times.

Look Inward How I feel in my body right now is . . . inhale through your nose . . . exhale through your nose.

Being around sick people makes me feel . . . inhale . . . exhale . . .

When my body isn't at its best, it makes me feel . . . inhale . . . exhale . . .

Letting go of resistance to ALL healing now makes me feel . . . inhale . . . exhale . . .

Emit Hum three times.

Activate See it! Visualize an image of healing light such as a bright shining star or a stream of golden sunlight.

Nourish Feel it! Imagine what it would feel like to be in the presence of such a beautiful healing light. How it might open you up to possibilities.

Surrender Say: "I allow healing. I allow light. I allow feeling. I allow processing. I allow relief. I allow renewal."

Ease Say: "I am healing. I am feeling. I am processing. I am light. I am relief. I am renewal. I am free."

Cleansing
Perfectionism

Do you have exacting standards? Do you tend to be critical of yourself and others? Or perhaps you strive to be faultless and get down on yourself for even the smallest error. Perfectionism can arise from an internal need for love and approval, messages of inadequacy during childhood, or it could be your style of managing your life. You like things to be a certain way and in some cases that could help you be successful, yet here is the thing, sometimes you might get so caught up in the details or putting things in order that you actually miss the things that matter. Things like how your wants and needs may or may not be met by others. For example, are you finding people around you are getting a little offended, feeling unheard, or maybe taking things a little personally? While you can't control how other people feel, what you can do is CLEANSE your need to have things go an exact way as this may be a subconscious means of suppressing your emotions.

Clear Reactivity Using your fingertips, scratch and rub your scalp in the way you would when washing your hair vigorously with shampoo. Do this for about thirty seconds. Pause and breathe.

Look Inward How I feel in my body right now is . . . inhale through your nose . . . exhale through your nose.

When things are out of order, it makes me feel . . . inhale . . . exhale . . .

Looking like I'm in control of my appearance and environment makes me feel . . . inhale . . . exhale . . .

When I notice flaws and imperfections, it makes me feel . . . inhale . . . exhale . . .

Emit Hum three times.

Activate See it! Visualize an image of wholeness, release, and unlocking. Perhaps a scene in which you see yourself undoing the latch on a doorway that opens into a vast, green, beautiful landscape.

Nourish Feel it! Walk through that doorway now as you expand yourself beyond the walls of insecurity, fear, and doubt. Let your heart lead the way.

Surrender Say: "I allow release. I allow connection. I allow security. I allow trust. I allow healing. I allow wholeness."

Ease Say: "I am whole. I am trusting. I am enough. I am transformation. I am free."

Cleansing Exhaustion

Do you struggle with fatigue or overtiredness? And because of this do you find yourself lying or sitting down a lot during the day or taking a break to the point where it's interfering with your life or your appreciation of things, like taking a walk on a beautiful day? Or maybe you have coped with your fatigue by reaching for an energy drink, cup of coffee, late-night snack, or too much television. While it is important to let your doctor know about what you have been feeling, fatigue can also be caused by reacting to the emotional energy of other people and events. Just like a cold can be contagious, so can emotions, and if you have been watching too much news lately or you have someone in your life that has been being a bit demanding or judgmental, consider finding alternative ways to support yourself through fatigue. Things like taking deep breaths, eating foods rich in vitamin B, spending a little time in the sunlight to stimulate your pituitary gland, or increasing cardiovascular exercise can give you a boost. Use this CLEANSE to clear any unprocessed emotions or energy you might have contracted from others and see if it doesn't put a little pep in your step!

Clear Reactivity Certain scents such as lavender, lemon oil, or pine are an effective way to promote emotional processing and non-synthetic blends of essential oils are a good way to enjoy them. The best way to do this is put a dab on a cotton ball and inhale . . . and exhale . . . through your nose as you breathe it in. If you do not have any oils, you can imagine smelling a fragrance or cutting open a fresh orange or lemon.

Look Inward How I feel in my body right now is . . . inhale through your nose . . . exhale through your nose.

Smelling this now makes me feel . . . inhale . . . exhale . . .

Breathing this scent in and out right now makes me feel . . . inhale . . . exhale . . .

Emit Hum three times.

Activate See it! Visualize your senses waking up to the sun, fresh air, and a light breeze.

Nourish Feel it! Imagine the breeze blowing your hair, skimming your scalp, or cooling your spirit.

Surrender Say: "I allow fresh. I allow alert. I allow active. I allow renewal. I allow rejuvenation."

Ease Say: "I am fresh. I am renewed. I am alert. I am breathing. I am energized. I am free."

Cleansing Cravings

We have all been there, telling ourselves we are going to start
eating healthy, give up the chips and sweets in hopes that we
can create a more balanced diet and lifestyle. A craving is a powerful
desire for something: a need, want, or yearning. It's not just about
snacks and food—we can also crave sex, alcohol, or attention. We
might have such a burning desire to fall in love or to get out of a
troubling relationship that this manifests as a craving.

The challenge is how do we handle a craving? In terms of your
health, you may find eating nutritious food is one thing, but dealing
with those unwanted cravings can be a whole different ball game. In
terms of well-being, you might know how to make the situation better
but cannot release yourself from the yearning. So to help you, let
me ask you this question: Could your cravings be a sign that you are
losing energy? Not just physical energy, but the energy you can gain
from your emotions when they are processed. If you are someone who

struggles with cravings, step one of the CLEANSE will always be an important one.

Clear Reactivity Taking a probiotic supplement or eating a food that contains probiotics like yogurt, pickles, or sourdough bread can help tone your vagus nerve. Some people swear by the benefits of adding apple cider vinegar to their morning routine. (You can even mix it with some water to make it a little easier on your system.) After you have given yourself a little probiotic boost, sit down, pause, and move on to step two.

Look Inward How I feel in my body right now is . . . inhale through your nose . . . exhale through your nose.

Having these urges inside me now makes me feel . . . inhale . . . exhale . . .

When I push away or resist these desires, I feel . . . inhale . . . exhale . . .

Emit Hum three times.

Activate See it! Visualize an image of light, freedom, enthusiasm, or desire. What do you see? Perhaps an image of what it would feel like to take off a backpack full of books. Rather than carry the weight of the books, instead you are able to sit down and enjoy reading them.

Nourish Feel it! Feel desire and enthusiasm in your body. Does it feel warm, expansive?

Surrender Say: "I allow movement. I allow passion. I allow desire. I allow release. I allow freedom."

Ease Say: "I am releasing. I am passionate. I am desire. I am energy. I am acceptance. I am free."

Cleansing Inflammation

Inflammation is a physical response to a wound or injury. It is part of your body's way of fighting off diseases, protecting, and healing you. However, when inflammation goes on too long and becomes chronic it can overtake your life. Rather than addressing the underlying causes (such as previous injuries) you may instead find yourself consumed by the symptoms (like back or joint pain). To heal, your cells require proper care, nutrition, hydration, sleep, and exercise. Without support, the inflammation can have damaging effects on your heart and arteries, and increase your risk for certain diseases.

It's a two-way street. My work with clients has shown me how unprocessed emotions can lead to physical pain (like neck aches), which can allow inflammation to arise. Either way, inflammation is something we want to avoid.

In the middle of this CLEANSE—usually around step two—it is not unusual for a tightness to arise, especially in your upper body, but this will soon be relieved by step three (the hum). If you suffer from inflammation, consider adding this into your self-care routine.

Clear Reactivity Begin with sound. Inhale through your nose . . . and on the exhale make the sound "yam." Draw it out for the entire exhale so it will be more like "yammmmmm." Repeat three times in a row—inhaling . . . and exhaling with a "yam," dispersing this vibration throughout your entire body.

Look Inward How I feel in my body right now is . . . inhale through your nose . . . exhale through your nose.

Feeling this way right now makes me feel . . . inhale . . . exhale . . .

Releasing and healing these injuries now makes me feel . . . inhale . . . exhale . . .

When I release the need to protect myself, it makes me feel . . . inhale . . . exhale . . .

Emit Hum three times.

Activate See it! Visualize light colors—greens, pinks, yellows—circulating throughout your body now.

Nourish Feel it! Let the light bounce inside you, playfully, gently, and softly.

Surrender Say: "I allow healing. I allow release. I allow soft. I allow freedom. I allow soothing. I allow ease."

Ease Say: "I am well. I am healthy. I am safe. I am comfort. I am joy."

Cleansing a Tough Diagnosis

One of my earliest clients contacted me virtually from the other side of the world. She had just received the tough and frightening diagnosis of breast cancer and was looking to connect with professionals who worked with mind-body healing. I like to believe the CLEANSE brought us together. It would be through this client that I first learned the shock, sadness, and fear that comes along with a medical diagnosis and I'm so grateful to have been able to be part of her healing process. Since then I have worked with individuals who are looking for support in dealing with their diagnosis or that of a loved one. So many tough things, including dementia, cancer, heart disease, or Parkinson's, and each is difficult to hear, live with, and digest emotionally especially before you have a plan of action. Entering the medical world in this way is like signing up for the master's degree you never asked for—you are going to learn a lot about treatments and protocols, and there will be terms and explanations you may not understand. As you go through the process, this CLEANSE can be a meaningful part of your journey.

Clear Reactivity Using the fingers of both hands, feel the back of your scalp close to the nape of your neck. You will find two soft indentations where the lower part of your skull meets the top portion of your neck. Press your fingers gently as you massage these fascia or connective tissues. If you start to relax or settle into your breath, you know you have the right spot. After doing this for about a minute, rest your hands, roll your shoulders a couple of times, and move to step two.

Look Inward How I feel in my body right now is . . . inhale through your nose . . . exhale through your nose.

Having this diagnosis brought to my attention made me feel . . . inhale . . . exhale . . .

Leaving the conversation with the doctor made me feel . . . inhale . . . exhale . . .

Having this situation, come up for me or my loved one now makes me feel . . . inhale . . . exhale . . .

Emit Hum three times slowly, allowing three-second pauses between each hum.

Activate See it! Visualize an image of comfort, relief, health, benefits, support, and aid. Perhaps an image of the lush and verdant rain forest or a basketful of some of Mother Nature's natural remedies such as aloe vera, chamomile, and coconut.

Nourish Feel it! Touch these healing gifts from nature. What would aloe feel like in your hands (even if it is not something you need)?

Surrender Say: "I allow healing. I allow resonating. I allow purpose. I allow relief. I allow love."

Ease Say: "I am love. I am comfort. I am health. I am strong. I am supported. I am free."

Cleansing Physical Tension

Muscle tension is your body's response to extreme levels of stress. For example, if you suffer from chronic headaches or migraines your body may have a pattern of responding to stress by stiffening your shoulders, which will cause the muscles in your neck, jaw, and top of your skull to tighten up. Sometimes this tension arises in our bodies as backaches or foot cramps. If you experience chronic muscle tension it is important to have relaxation techniques built into your daily life, like the one you will find in this CLEANSE. In addition, I have found through my work that individuals with muscle tension tend to have exaggerated thoughts. In other words, they get "stuck" in fearful or negative thoughts that magnify if they aren't processed, and so I have addressed these in this CLEANSE.

Clear Reactivity In this CLEANSE you'll clear reactivity by trying the progressive muscle relaxation technique (PMRT). Sitting up tall in a chair, make fists with your hands, squeezing to the point where the muscles in your hands, face, shoulders, and legs tighten up. Hold this tension for five seconds . . . one . . . two . . . three . . . four . . . five . . . and release. Notice how your blood begins to circulate and flow. Repeat two or three times in a row.

Look Inward How I feel in my body right now is . . . inhale through your nose . . . exhale through your nose. As you breathe, make sure to draw your navel in fully toward your spine before you inhale.

When my thoughts are magnified, it makes me feel . . . inhale . . . exhale . . .

Startling myself by releasing tension in the second part of PMRT makes me feel . . . inhale . . . exhale . . .

When I quiet my mind, it makes me feel . . . inhale . . . exhale . . .

Feeling present now makes me feel . . . inhale . . . exhale . . .

Emit Hum three times.

Activate See it! Visualize an image of something that is grounding, centered, calm, present, and connected. The way the trunk of a giant tree extends its roots deep down into the earth.

Nourish Feel it! Imagine standing next to that tree now and running your hands across the bark. Feel the rough texture and power beneath it.

Surrender Say: "I allow presence. I allow connection. I allow relaxation. I allow calm. I allow nourishment."

Ease Say: "I am nourishment. I am present. I am rooted. I am strong. I am free."

Cleansing
Sedentary Behavior

We're sedentary when we allow ourselves to sit or lay in one spot for prolonged periods of time without stretching, activity, or movement. While it can be fun and therapeutic to have a day where you binge on movies, eat popcorn, and barely move from your couch, when once in a while becomes a lifestyle, especially for those of us who must spend much of our days at our desks, this can create physical and emotional imbalances. For one, your body is meant to move, and it *needs* to move to be able to stay strong and resilient. Today, in part thanks to our ability to access pretty much everything via the internet, sedentary behavior is becoming chronic. According to experts, reducing the incidence of health conditions such as heart disease and diabetes means taking more physical steps. Most adults get in about three thousand steps per day when we really ought to be aiming for ten thousand.[8] Yikes! We can help ourselves meet this quota by parking farther away from our destination, taking the stairs instead of the elevator, and walking or riding our bikes. It is all about the steps, and it's also about this CLEANSE.

Clear Reactivity Today (as long as you are not pregnant) breathe in and then release three to five sharp exhales. Your tummy will pull in tautly. You might even hear yourself make a sound (such as "whoosh") when you do this. The point is to stimulate your abdominal muscles while releasing any stale carbon dioxide. After repeating this three to five times, pause and breathe through your nose . . . inhale . . . and exhale . . . and now move to step two.

Look Inward How I feel in my body right now is . . . inhale through your nose . . . exhale through your nose.

The idea of getting up and going for a walk when I'm tired or busy makes me feel . . . inhale . . . exhale . . .

Having to move more makes me feel . . . inhale . . . exhale . . .

Not moving or exercising makes me feel . . . inhale . . . exhale . . .

Emit Hum three times.

Activate See it! Visualize an image of playfulness, carefree fun, and ease. Perhaps an image of squirrels chasing each other among the branches, or yourself playing basketball or swimming in a lake.

Nourish Feel it! Imagine how one of these activities would feel. Imagine holding the ball in your hands right now and throwing it in the air. How might you feel the movement of energy in your belly?

Surrender Say: "I allow movement. I allow play. I allow exercise. I allow blood flow. I allow physicality. I allow freedom."

Ease Say: "I am moving. I am physical. I am energized. I am strong. I am resilient. I am free."

Part VI

CRISIS & TRAGEDY

Traumatic experiences and memories can also benefit from a CLEANSE as we seek help and learn to address and work through and with the pain. Remember it is not as much a matter of getting over as getting through.

Whenever it feels like things are falling apart, being connected to the vibration of the CLEANSE provides me and so many of my friends, family members, and clients with a sense of comfort, a starting point as we cope and heal. It is through these practices I return to a state of faith, love, trust, hope, and so much more. Perhaps it is the structure these seven steps apply and the reliability that you will receive energetic comfort as you move through and rewrite your story. During the toughest of times a CLEANSE can be a reliable resource and first step in self-care.

During the summer of the COVID-19 pandemic and the events following the tragic death of George Floyd, reactivity was the highest I had seen in my lifetime. Even the mellowest people were anxious and upset. Suddenly schools were closed and we were all wearing masks, stories of suffering filled the news, and we all faced shortages and health and financial insecurity. People were scared, uncertain, and worried about their futures. During this time I turned to the one thing I knew could help, the CLEANSE. I formed a virtual group of twelve individuals and together we moved through the process. Together with my "spiritual warriors" we shared our experiences and insights—the things they reported feeling, seeing, and hearing were like messages from heaven. When we cleansed there is no doubt in my mind we became conduits for bringing vibrations of peace and love to earth.

Someday we will look back and realize our emotions (when processed) were enough.

Cleansing Being Overwhelmed by the Suffering of Others

Suffering on our planet is a real and unfortunate part of life. While some people are more readily able to mourn and recover from tragedies and crises or even harden to them, others can become so overwhelmed by what they see, hear, and imagine that they become paralyzed. You know you are overwhelmed by the suffering of others if you begin to feel emotionally and physically depleted. Some people report feeling like they literally have weights on their shoulders, while others experience it as a crushing mental pressure.

Perhaps it is partially due to the bombardment of news and social media creating an avalanche of information and unfiltered misery.

It seems as if there is less time in between one upsetting piece of news and the next to recover and gain strength. No wonder you likely feel overwhelmed at times. While shutting down some of your media consumption (or at least limiting exposure) can help, it is important that when you start to feel overwhelmed, you take some time to CLEANSE.

Before you begin, I think you ought to know something the CLEANSE has taught me: suffering can actually be a way of coping. In other words, there may be a part of you that suffers as a way to deal with and process your sense of being overwhelmed. For example, you may find yourself sitting in the energy of suffering, succumbing to the burdens it can bring. Sounds strange but true. This will make more sense to you after the CLEANSE.

Clear Reactivity Certain scents are an effective way to promote emotional processing and non-synthetic blends of essential oils are a good way to enjoy them. I recommend lavender or bergamot root for this CLEANSE. Rub a drop of oil between your hands, take a nice inhale as you sit up tall and allow the fragrance to travel into your nose and throughout your body. Then, take the remaining oil on your hands and rub the back of your neck. If you do not have any oils, you can imagine smelling these scents or maybe brew yourself a cup of Earl Grey tea and inhale the bergamot.

Look Inward How I feel in my body right now is . . . inhale through your nose . . . exhale through your nose.

Witnessing suffering on the planet makes me feel . . . inhale . . . exhale . . .

Hearing, knowing, and imagining suffering makes me feel . . . inhale . . . exhale . . .

When I turn to suffering as a way to cope, it makes me feel . . . inhale . . . exhale . . .

Emit Hum five times and as you do, acknowledge how you are releasing the ways you might be holding on to suffering to suppress your emotions.

Activate See it! Visualize an image of joy, comfort, peace, happiness, and freedom. This may be an image from nature—perhaps children playing in the ocean waves, birds swooping and soaring, or whatever else shows up in your mind's eye.

Nourish Feel it! What would it feel like to have this energy moving through your body? What sensations might rise up in you?

Surrender Say: "I allow joy. I allow resilience. I allow energy. I allow relief. I allow comfort. I allow healing."

Ease Say: "I am joyous. I am resilient. I am energy. I am relief. I am comfort. I am healing. I am free . . . we are free. I can use the strength I find in this freedom to help others."

Cleansing
Helplessness

During the early days of COVID-19, my friend complained to me about her husband. "He is always venting to me about the news," she said. "It drives me nuts and then I end up getting irritated and moody with him." As we moved through this CLEANSE she discovered the ways her husband's style for dealing with his own feelings of powerlessness and helplessness (not to mention a world in crisis) reminded her of what it was like living with her father on a daily basis. Although she loved her father immensely, his reactive style defaulting immediately into helplessness at times felt threatening and oppressive. Once my friend made this connection she understood why she got so triggered and this in itself calmed her down. Now she could view the situation from a place of compassion for herself and her husband. Let's CLEANSE.

Clear Reactivity Imagine a straw inside a glass full of water. Heck, let's make it good—how about a milkshake? Visualize liquid going up and down that straw. Now imagine your spine is a straw, and visualize cerebral spinal fluid moving from your lower spine all the way up to the nape of your neck. Massage this point, which is one of the paths of your vagus nerve.

Look Inward How I feel in my body right now is . . . inhale through your nose . . . exhale through your nose.

When my energy diminishes, it makes me feel . . . inhale . . . exhale . . .

When other people's energy diminishes, it makes me feel . . . inhale . . . exhale . . .

Emit Hum three or four times. Be sure to take a nice long inhale before you exhale your hum.

Activate See it! Visualize an image of expansiveness. You might see the ocean, stars in the sky, or mountains.

Nourish Feel it! Imagine being in that expansive space. How would you know you were there? What would you sense and feel inside and outside of yourself?

Surrender Say: "I allow expansiveness. I allow growth. I allow strength. I allow release. I allow understanding. I allow freedom."

Ease Say: "I am power. I am strength. I am expansive. I am infinite. I am possibility. I am calm. I am free."

Cleansing Fear
of Contracting
Illness

We have all been there—that moment you take your seat in an airplane or board the bus and the person behind you starts to cough and blow their nose. Or worse yet the parent of the kid your child just played with suddenly comes down with a fever. While these things are part of life, and let's face it, germs get passed around, in the case of pandemics like the coronavirus, or an influenza outbreak, the mere thought of being exposed can cause you well-founded anxiety. The thing is, fear isn't going to keep you healthy and may even weaken your immune system.

Let's break this down. Is it your fear of being sick or going through the experience of having the symptoms? Perhaps it is fear of not having enough immunity or physical strength to take care of yourself or your family. Maybe you are worried about being a carrier and giving it to someone else. Nonetheless, take the necessary precautions, wash your hands, cover your cough, keep your distance, get rest, eat well, and do not forget to CLEANSE.

Clear Reactivity Sit up nice and tall with your chin parallel to the earth and shoulders back and dropped. Slowly inhale through your nose as you inflate the sides of your waist for a count of one . . . two . . . three . . . and now (unless you are pregnant) hold your breath for a count of count of one . . . two . . . three. Slowly exhale for a count of one . . . two . . . three . . . as you draw your navel toward your spine. Repeat two or three times in a row.

Look Inward How I feel in my body right now is . . . inhale through your nose . . . exhale through your nose.

Being around sickness makes me feel . . . inhale . . . exhale . . .

The thought of contracting illness makes me feel . . . inhale . . . exhale . . .

Emit Hum three times.

Activate See it! Visualize an image of something mild, pleasant, delightful, and happy. Perhaps the way light bounces and dapples on a body of water like a river or the leaves of a tree as its branches sway gently in the breeze.

Nourish Feel it! Imagine the light you see tenderly bouncing inside of you and moving the energy just enough for you to begin to feel calm and relief.

Surrender Say: "I allow tenderness. I allow calm. I allow mildness. I allow pleasant. I allow resilience. I allow carefree. I allow freedom."

Ease Say: "I am happy. I am strong. I am resilient. I am capable. I am love. I am health. I am free."

Cleansing Fear of
Death

You may look at this CLEANSE and think to yourself I know I have it, but there's no way you're going to CLEANSE it. If so, I totally get it—fear of our death and the death of others is a scary subject because so much is unknown. When I was eight years old my mother had a mild heart attack. I remember watching her walk around the house with a heart monitor, and I was consumed by thoughts of her dying. *What would I do? How would I live?* While these types of responses are common, without a CLEANSE, they can manifest into behaviors such as being overly attached or clingy or even paralysis in terms of living our own lives. While making good choices such as wearing your seat belt, careful driving, not smoking, and keeping up with your doctors' appointments can extend your days and maybe even years, worrying or fearing loss can contribute to elevated levels of anxiety not to mention put quite a bit of strain on your relationships.

Clear Reactivity Make a fist with one or both hands, grip tightly, and hold for three seconds. Release. Repeat this action a few more times—gripping and releasing. As you do, notice how this action induces the relaxation response.

Look Inward How I feel in my body right now is . . . inhale through your nose . . . exhale through your nose.

Having these fearful thoughts makes me feel . . . inhale . . . exhale . . .

Releasing these fears now makes me feel . . . inhale . . . exhale . . . slowly through your nose.

Emit Hum three to five times.

Activate See it! Visualize durability, vitality, safety, strength, and thriving. Maybe a beautiful stone or crystal, a piece of metal, or polished wood.

Nourish Feel it! What would that durable object feel like if you held it in your hands?

Surrender Say: "*I allow!* I allow durability. I allow safety. I allow thriving. I allow presence. I allow strength. I allow freedom."

Ease Say: "I am safe. I am durable. I am here. I am now. I am free. I am breath."

Cleansing Witnessing or Being the Subject of Abuse or Violence

Have you noticed when something violent or awful happens in the world it gets replayed by news channels and social media outlets dozens of times? Each instance of witnessing a violent or abusive event, either on television, your phone, or in person has an impact on your psyche and this is multiplied many times when it is happening to you. If you are currently around someone who is verbally, physically, or emotionally abusive, please get help right away!

Reach out to a professional in your community such as a therapist or local shelter that can keep you safe. What you may not know is there are civilians and social workers at many police stations who can inform and guide you as you work through things like harassment and restraining orders.

If you need help, get it as soon as possible and then CLEANSE! If you feel stuck, paralyzed, or numb from what you have been exposed to in the media or on a lower level (like a mean-spirited coworker or encountering road rage) spend some time with this CLEANSE now.

Clear Reactivity Pour a glass of cool water and take some slow sips. It is important your body feels hydrated and safe. After a few mouthfuls, sit up tall and exhale by pulling your navel toward your spine . . . one . . . two . . . three. As you do this soften your face and jaw.

Look Inward How I feel in my body right now is . . . inhale through your nose . . . exhale through your nose.

When I realize the impact these images and events have on me, it makes me feel . . . inhale . . . exhale . . .

Having these experiences in my body now makes me feel . . . inhale . . . exhale . . .

Emit Sit up tall, inhale through your nose, and then exhale as you open your mouth wide and chant a long, slow hum. Pause for three seconds in between hums. Repeat this as many times as feels right for you.

Activate See it! Visualize gentleness, kindness, love, safety, compassion, and peace. What would you see? Perhaps a dove, morning dew sparkling on green grass, or a quiet night sky.

Nourish Feel it! Imagine touching your visualization. What would the dew feel like on your fingertips? Breathe into this experience now.

Surrender Say: "I allow peace. I allow kindness. I allow love. I allow safety. I allow compassion. I allow trust. I allow freedom."

Ease Say: "I am peaceful. I am trusting. I am kind. I am lovable. I am purifying. I am safe. I am secure. I am free."

Cleansing Global Financial Crisis

From 1929 to 1939, America and the world faced one of its most significant economic crises—the Great Depression. The financial industry collapsed, unemployment was at an all-time high, and many people lost their homes, went hungry, or were forced to ration their food. Since then, there have been several other incidences where people have experienced financial losses and the stock market has crashed or dipped resulting in significant losses or even the obliteration of savings and retirement plans. The impact of these crises does not disappear and can impact generations—so the anxiety can be simultaneously long and short term. Without a CLEANSE, the distress around these incidents and money (becoming a "have" or a "have-not") becomes divisive, a way to determine who has power and influence and who does not. I like to think of this CLEANSE as cleaning our energetic history, removing all the impurities, fears, and misuses of financial power as we make the best of our current situation.

Clear Reactivity The sound of "lam" is a powerful one and when repeated, sends a vibration to your root or pelvic area. Energetically this is an area of the body that is believed to hold much of our history, heredities, and patterns. Repeat the "lam" sound aloud five times in a row.

Look Inward How I feel in my body right now is . . . inhale through your nose . . . exhale through your nose.

Releasing this history now makes me feel . . . inhale . . . exhale . . .

Relinquishing this fear from my body now makes me feel . . . inhale . . . exhale . . .

Emit Hum five times.

Activate See it! Visualize an image in nature of wealth, worth, abundance, and resources. Perhaps a large redwood tree or an expansive view of the ocean.

Nourish Feel it! Picture yourself standing at the base of that giant redwood and feel the solidity of the earth beneath your feet, the protection and security the leaves, branches, and even trunk provide.

Surrender Say: "I allow expansion. I allow security. I allow growth. I allow prosperity. I allow freedom. I allow ease. I allow wealth. I allow value. I allow worth."

Ease Say: "I am worthy. I am valued. I am abundant. I am prosperity. I am wealth. I am in flow. I am free."

Cleansing Hatred and Racism

When I asked my client what he wanted to CLEANSE he replied, "The dark side of humanity."

"What do you mean?" I inquired.

He continued with "Hatred, racism, violence, all of it." It was clear what had been happening in the world was weighing on him that day and he described it as an oppressive feeling he couldn't see past or through—he literally felt the weight on his shoulders. Here is what came through his CLEANSE: hatred and racism are heavily intertwined with suppressed emotions of shame and withdrawal. These painful feelings can be exacerbated by the guilt that is often connected to them and can endure through generations. When these emotions show up in the body to be cleared it can bring on a sense of hopelessness, sorrow, and depression and may even lead to self-harm or substance abuse. The challenge is the body will do anything to get rid of these heavy sensations that are the result of experiencing or witnessing acts of violence and rage. This is because hatred does not match our true nature, but the CLEANSE method does.

Clear Reactivity Take your two peace-sign fingers and press about one inch above your navel while sitting up tall. Hold the press for a count of one . . . two seconds. Now move your fingers over about one inch to the right, press gently, and hold for a count of one . . . two. Finally, move your fingers over to the left about one inch from the center line above your navel press and hold for two more seconds. Relax your arms and breathe.

Look Inward How I feel in my body right now is . . . inhale through your nose . . . exhale through your nose.

Tuning in to this heaviness inside me now makes me feel . . . inhale . . . exhale . . .

Carrying these sensations makes me feel . . . inhale . . . exhale . . .

Emit Hum a minimum of three times. Visualize a pool of clear water as you hum. Imagine the water moving from the vibration of your hum.

Activate See it! Visualize the water swirling, trembling, and whirling as if it were running down into an eddy or down a drain.

Nourish Feel it! Touch the water, feel it on your hands, notice the sensation as it moves. Pay attention to the temperature of the water, the pressure, the weight, and the way it influences how you feel inside your body now.

Surrender Say: "I allow release. I allow heritage. I allow esteem. I allow respect. I allow value. I allow worth. I allow praise. I allow love. I allow freedom."

Ease Say: "I am released. I am transformed. I am proud. I am honored. I am respected. I am valued. I am worthy. I am free."

Cleansing
Extreme
Powerlessness

I t is one thing to feel a sense of powerless or loss of control within yourself, and it is a whole different ball game when you feel and sense it in others. If your community has been impacted by extreme circumstances such as a tragic death, natural disaster, or violence you may experience a loss of control. This can make you feel like there is a void or absence and maybe even a desperate hopelessness in your life. For example, you may feel like your voice doesn't matter or you are having a challenging time connecting with others. This can bring on fearful behaviors such as chronic worrying, suspicion, or a lack of trust in your community and its leaders. You may handle these feelings by withdrawing, becoming less social or by lashing out (like venting on social media). While you may be tempted to look to the external world to retrieve whatever it is you long for or miss, you won't attain it until you realize there is more power within you than outside.

Clear Reactivity Sit up nice and tall. Tilt your right ear toward your right shoulder, so you feel a stretch in your neck. Then move your left arm straight out to the side, which will intensify the stretch a bit. Breathe. Bring your head back to center, drop your arm, and repeat on the other side. This time lift your right arm out to the side to deepen your stretch. Release and receive your breath.

Look Inward How I feel in my body right now is . . . inhale through your nose . . . exhale through your nose.

Living in my community right now makes me feel . . . inhale . . . exhale . . .

When I feel my voice, opinions, or beliefs do not matter, it makes me feel . . . inhale . . . exhale . . .

When I can't connect to love, it makes me feel . . . inhale . . . exhale . . .

Emit Hum at least three times and ideally six or seven times.

Activate See it! Visualize an image of compassion, connection, and acceptance. Where would you go in your mind to connect to this vibration? Imagine that safe and peaceful space.

Nourish Feel it! Imagine what it would feel like to be in an environment where people were smiling, where even the trees and clouds radiated joy, and the flowers did as well. What would the atmosphere be like?

Surrender Say: "I allow kindness. I allow tender. I allow acceptance. I allow gentleness. I allow compassion. I allow love. I allow freedom."

Ease Say: "I am kind. I am tender. I am accepted. I am gentle. I am compassionate. I am love. I am free."

Cleansing Inequality and Injustice

Inequality is about disproportion. It is when resources are unfairly distributed within a community. When policies and decision are made in this way they can promote bias and prejudices. As result collective belief systems begin to develop, ones that contain elements of racism, prejudice, and bigotry. If we want to have conscious conversations regarding the injustices that exist within our society it can make a big difference if we CLEANSE together first. Otherwise we risk speaking from a place of reactivity. When we speak from reactivity we inevitably hold and spread negative emotional energy of fear, frustration, and anger. Reactivity does not transform energy, it inflames it. The more reactive we are the more separate and consequently unequal we become. By choosing to CLEANSE before we find a way to connect we raise our level of consciousness so we can begin to engage in conversations with our higher selves rather than the parts of us that feel broken, betrayed, denied, or wounded.

Clear Reactivity Here you'll practice a three-part breathing technique. For the first part, sit up tall and focus on your lower abdomen and pelvic area. The second part focuses on the center of your rib cage and heart. In the third part you will focus on your collarbones and upper chest. For each part, you inhale slowly through your nose, filling up the correlated part of the body. On the exhale, pull your navel in nice and slow as you continue to observe your upper, middle, and lower core. Repeat twice, and then move to step two.

Look Inward How I feel in my body right now is . . . inhale through your nose . . . exhale through your nose.

When things seem unfair or unequal, it makes me feel . . . inhale . . . exhale . . .

Seeing or having things function in an imbalanced way makes me feel . . . inhale . . . exhale . . .

Detaching from old systems now makes me feel . . . inhale . . . exhale . . .

Emit Hum three times.

Activate See it! Visualize an image of patterns or old agreements being released. You might see an ancient document being torn up and burned, or dissolved in a pool of pure water.

Nourish Feel it! Imagine the document representing old ways of thinking becoming saturated with cleansing water until it dissolves or evaporates into powerless smoke.

Surrender Say: "I allow liquidity. I allow diffusion. I allow breakdown. I allow melt."

Ease Say: "I am renewal. I am fluid. I am transformed. I am consciousness. I am change. I am free."

Cleansing While Waiting for Aid and Support

If you are currently waiting for some kind of assistance, whether it is medical or financial or related to housing so you can begin to rebuild your life, then you know how difficult it can be to process your emotions during this period. The anticipation alone (when left unprocessed) can cause you to feel nervous, worried, fearful, and unsettled. As a result you may have a sense of powerlessness, as if the fate of your future depends upon on the actions of a stranger or policies beyond your control.

I have seen top-notch students fail classes while waiting for a decision on their immigration status—the tremendous fear of being removed from their school due to an expired visa outweighed their ability to achieve. For others it may be waiting for an organ donor, approval on a loan, child support, or temporary housing after a disaster. Because each of these circumstances is inherently stressful, it will be important for you to CLEANSE. Otherwise, you might find your unprocessed emotions exacerbating your feelings and diminishing your overall sense of well-being, hope, and trust.

Clear Reactivity Sit in a chair with your feet hip-width apart and flat on the floor. Place your hands on the tops of your thighs as you gently tuck your chin and round your spine into a cat yoga posture and then exhale as you curve your spine. Inhale as you draw your shoulder blades back, lifting the front of your heart as you open up your chest and spine. Tuck again and exhale. Repeat two or three times in a row, then pause, sit up tall and be quiet for a moment before you move on to the next step.

Look Inward How I feel in my body right now is . . . inhale through your nose . . . exhale through your nose.

Sitting in this energy now makes me feel . . . inhale . . . exhale . . .

When I do not know what to expect, it makes me feel . . . inhale . . . exhale . . .

Being in the unknown makes me feel . . . inhale . . . exhale . . .

Emit Hum three times.

Activate See it! Visualize something that represents new beginnings, productivity, abundance, resourcefulness, and fertility. See it in nature—perhaps an apple or peach tree heavy with fruit.

Nourish Feel it! What would it feel like to be in that space? What does the fertile ground that supports the tree smell like? Are there birds supported by its branches? Pluck a piece of fruit and taste its nourishing sweetness.

Surrender Say: "I allow fertility. I allow growth. I allow expansion. I allow new beginnings. I allow endings. I allow completion. I allow freedom."

Ease Say: "I am new beginnings. I am unlimited possibilities. I am abundance. I am new growth. I am completion. I am free. I am love."

Bonus: Morning Cleanse

Each morning, I grab my favorite coffee mug, sit in a comfy chair, and move through this CLEANSE. With that said, it doesn't always look perfect. Sometimes the dog needs to go out and pee, one of my children interrupts me, or I find my thoughts wandering off. Yet, no matter what (and how many interruptions) I begin with the C and end with the E. It looks something like this.

Clear Reactivity Tilt your right ear toward your right shoulder, hold for four seconds, bring your head back to center, pause for five seconds, breathe and then tilt your left ear toward your left shoulder (hold for four seconds), bring your head back to center, breathe in and out through your nose, and then move to step two.

Look Inward How I feel in my body right now is . . . inhale through your nose . . . exhale through your nose.

Being in my body right now makes me feel . . . inhale . . . exhale . . .

Emit Hum two to three times in a row. Pause. Take an inhale and exhale.

Activate See it! Visualize calm. For me it is a lake I love to swim in near my mother's house.

Nourish Feel it! If I tune in I can feel the water and the smell of the air.

Surrender Say: "I allow calm, I allow trust, I allow release, I allow free, and I allow energy."

Ease Say: "I am calm, I am trust, I am grateful, I am free, and I am an infinite creator." I sit quietly for a few more minutes sipping my coffee, giving my emotions the time and space they need to fully process.

Notes

1. Guy Winch, "10 Surprising Facts About Rejection," *Psychology Today*, July 3, 2013, http://www.psychologytoday.com/us/blog/the-squeaky-wheel/201307/10-surprising-facts-about-rejection.

2. Katherine Ponte, "The Mental Health Movement in the Workplace," National Alliance on Mental Illness, June 10, 2020, https://www.nami.org/Blogs/NAMI-Blog/June-2020/The-Mental-Health-Movement-in-the-Workplace?utm_source=naminow.

3. Jeanne Meister, "The Future of Work: Job Hopping Is the 'New Normal' for Millennials," *Forbes*, January 3, 2017, https://www.forbes.com/sites/jeannemeister/2012/08/14/the-future-of-work-job-hopping-is-the-new-normal-for-millennials/.

4. Theo Tsaousides, "Why Are We Scared of Public Speaking?" *Psychology Today*, November 27, 2017, https://www.psychologytoday.com/us/blog/smashing-the-brainblocks/201711/why-are-we-scared-public-speaking.

5. National Institute of Neurological Disorders and Stroke, "Brain Basics: Understanding Sleep," accessed August 9,

2020, https://www.ninds.nih.gov/Disorders/Patient-Caregiver
-Education/Understanding-Sleep.

6. American Psychiatric Association, "What Is a Substance Use
   Disorder?," accessed August 9, 2020, https://www.psychiatry
   .org/patients-families/addiction/what-is-addiction.

7. Hilary Jacobs Hendel, "Ignoring Your Emotions Is Bad for
   Your Health. Here's What to Do About It," *Time*, February 27,
   2018, https://time.com/5163576/ignoring-your-emotions-bad
   -for-your-health/.

8. Sara Lindberg, "How Many Steps Do I Need a Day?" Health-
   line, March 8, 2019, https://www.healthline.com/health/how
   -many-steps-a-day.

Acknowledgments

Thank you to my husband for your love, support, wisdom, and laughter. I love you. Cheers to twenty-three years for us! To my kind, brave, beautiful mother, Judy. To my three daughters, Megan, Mikayla, and Makenzie, whom I love with all my heart and who manage to put up with all this CLEANSE talk. To my father, for your gentle heart and spirit. To Alice Peck, my editor: What I can I say, you have been a bit of an angel in my life. Thank you for your talent, honesty, professionalism, and love. To Steve Harris, my agent, I will forever hold these words you once wrote to me close to my heart: "Sherianna, I think I fell in love (not with you, although you are pretty great) with the CLEANSE." To my support team—Jason Peterson, Ben Biddick, Christine Darby, Dan Riordan, Kerensa Ransom, Mark Gough, and Gillian Hurrie—thank you for your talent, efficiency, and commitment to helping me get this world feeling again. To the whole team at St. Martin's Press, particularly Gwen, who has been a pure pleasure to work with. Thank you all so much. To Elizabeth Guarino, Emily A. Francis,

Linda Mackenzie (owner of healthylife.net), and Jay (Emotional Detox Radio producer) for your professionalism and encouragement. Finally, to the students of the CLEANSE, for your honest feedback, validation, beautiful emotions, and vulnerability. Thank you all!

Resources and Ways to Connect

Resources

To learn more and have a deeper experience with the CLEANSE visit:

www.sheriannaboyle.com
www.emotionaldetoxnow.com
To Find:
Emotional Detox Coaching®
Cleanse Yoga®
Emotional Detox Podcast
Workshops & Retreats led by Sherianna

Follow

Instagram: @sherianna.boyle
Facebook: @sheriannaboyle
Twitter: Emotional Detox@sheriannaboyle
Youtube: https://www.youtube.com/c/SheriannaBoyle

Join

www.emotionaldetoxnow.com
CLEANSE live with Sherianna and a community of CLEANSErs!

About the Author

Jason Peterson

Sherianna Boyle is the author of nine books, founder of Emotional Detox Coaching®, the Cleanse Method®, and Cleanse Yoga®. She is an adjunct psychology professor, and a featured presenter at established centers such as Kripalu Center for Yoga & Health, 1440 Multiversity, and PESI Behavioral Health. Her *Emotional Detox* podcast and radio show have been listed in the top ten for downloads. Her books, coaching services, and resources can be found at www.sheriannaboyle.com and www.emotionaldetoxnow.com.